AF345845

wisdoms of the heart

WISDOMS OF THE HEART

Mudhakara of the
Shaykh Sidi Mohamed Faouzi al-Karkari

Translated by **Najat Ouhraich**

LES 7 LECTURES

Wisdoms of the Heart is published by the nonprofit organization
Anwar and his publishing house Les 7 Lectures

44 Fernand Brunfaut Street
1080 Brussels, Belgium

© Les 7 Lectures, 2022
All rights reserved

ISBN: 978-2-930978-72-7
Deposit number: D/2022/14.291/08 (Belgium)
Legal Deposit: December 2022

أعوذ بالله من الشيطان الرجيم

بسم الله الرحمن الرحيم

بسم الله الرحمن الرحيم

بسم الله الرحمن الرحيم

بسم الله

بسم الله

بسم الله

الله

الله

الله

ولا حول ولا قوة إلا بالله العلي العظيم

Table of Contents

Foreword

In the name of Allâh,
the Entirely Merciful,
the Especially Merciful.

All praise to Allâh, Lord of the worlds, the possessor of royalty and power, the First before all things and the Last after all things. Him whose appearance is so intense that He was veiled from the sight of creatures and whose occultation is so deep that the intellects collapsed in His presence.

And may the prayers and greetings be upon the Beloved, our Master, the Lord of the two worlds, *sayiduna* Muhammad. The seal of the prophets, the jewel of mercy and the heart of existence.

By the *baraka* of Sidi Shaykh Mohamed Fouzi al-Karkari, may Allâh sanctify His secret, knower by Allâh, reviver of faith, prophetic heir, *waliy* of Allâh, provider of divine Lights in the hearts of lovers.

We have, by the grace of our Shaykh Sidi Mohamed Faouzi al-Karkari, may Allâh sanctify his secret, gathered in the present work, passages of reminders. Translated for the first time from Arabic to French by the disciple Adrien Zapata, who spent a great number of years at his side.

The purpose of this book is to make these wisdoms accessible to English speakers and thus help wayfarer in their pathway.

We hope that our hearts will be receptive to his wisdoms and that our minds will be able to detect the secrets of his words... May Allâh open our chests and allow us to know Him and to know the Love, the love of the True, the One.

What is love?

In the beginning, it is a desire which becomes ardent in the heart, and how the lover falls in love, little by little, with the beloved. He recognizes and contemplates the beauty of the beloved in everything; to the point where the beloved becomes more important than everything in the world. It is in that sense, the Messenger of Allâh ﷺ was imploring: *"Ô Allâh, I am asking your love, the love of the one who love you as well as the work which will permit me to reach you love. Ô Allâh, make your love dearer to me than my own person, than my family, and than fresh water."*[1]

It is said that Qays Ibn al-Mulawwah had kissed between the eyes of the dog that used to roam around his beloved's house. When he had been asked about this, he answered: "I kiss its eyes because they saw Layla."

Then comes the appearance or the theophany of the beloved which is never separated from the Origin (*'ain*). This is how the image of the beloved comes to never again escape the eye of the lover, due to the stripping of his heart of all other except Him. Regarding the heart (*qalb*), it is only named for its changing nature (*yataqallab*) regarding the deep meanings it contains.

....

1   At-Tirmidhiy.

Then, the image of the beloved comes to pulverize all apparent forms residing in the heart of the beloved, so that it ends up not suffering from any reversal, except in the multiplicity of appearances of his beloved's beauty.

Then comes evanescence (*fana*) in actions, so that he saw things only as arising from the actions and from the harmonious arrangement wanted by the beloved. Then his heart becomes calm and quiet in the knowledge of the fundamental Origin of the act, so that deprivation and gift, health and sickness, wealth and poverty become equal to him.

Then comes evanescence (*fana*) in the Name, whereby the lover loses his "him" so that he only evokes the Name of his beloved. Thus, when *sayiduna* al-Hallâj came to a market and people asked him what he wanted, he replied "Allâh" and if people asked him about what he wanted to eat, he replied "Allâh". Thus, he had not any others answers except the mention of his beloved's Name and did not see anything else in the existence except the letters of his Name.

Finally, comes the evanescence (*fana*) on the beloved's Essence: where the heart penetrates the sacred place of love, and it moves towards the Ka'ba of passion. It no longer sees anyone in existence other than its beloved. Thus, when Layla's fool has been asked "Who are you?", he answered "I am Layla!" His whole being had dissipated in the love and passion he had for her. So much so, that he could only see in himself the one he loved.[2]

....

2   Extract of the book *The White Way* (المحجــة البيضــاء) by Sidi Shaykh Mohamed Faouzi al-Karkari.

The love by the touch

If you touch someone you love, for example, by shaking his hands, by this touch, you will spread in him a warmth. Then, when you look up to him, you will see a tear flowing on his right eye. Not the left eye, no... the right eye.

However, if you touch him with hate, and then look up to his face, you will find it obscured. And if your hate swells beyond the limit, you will see a tear flowing on his left eye. So be careful before you touch, you must pay specific attention to your inner state.

Regarding the shaking of hands, you will certainly think to the hadith:

"When the believer meets another believer, addresses him with the salam, takes his hand and shakes it, their sins scatter as the leaves of a tree scatter."[3]

For us, shaking hands refers to the *bay'a*, so when you come to take the *bay'a*, we, we love you and we touch you with a loving touch. It is not comparable to the touch that you do! When we put our hand in yours, we put it with heat, strong desire, with a spiritual flow of life and scarcely we tell you: "close your eyes and ignore your being", the Light of the Lord comes to blind you.

Why? Because our touch is not like yours.

....

3   Reported by at-Tabarânî in *Al-Awsat*.

Regarding you, when you touch us, you want to put forth your "masculinity" so you shake hands firmly because you are just a corporal idol with flesh and bones. It is like if you wanted to tell us: "I am strong, look my hand, *masha Allâh*... I have a working hand!" You have to know that it will take you away more than it will bond you.

In the *tariqa*, the physical force will not benefit you. If the physical force was important in your progression, you would not find the Shaykh suffering from multiple diseases, you would not find sick prophets nor soft and friendly messengers... On the contrary, you would find them strict, hard, brutal... yet these characteristics, are found with Pharaon and Haman.

The truth is your physical force is useful only when you go out looking for subsistence, working and bringing back food to your family. However, when you go out looking for an esoteric link with celestial worlds, forget this force and this hardness in your body and in your nature. Rather, oversee to establish and to asset the *haqiqa* of the love.

You pretend to stay up in the last third of the night doing your adoration, but if you really stayed awake in the last third of the night, we would not see you hard and unpleasant in the rest of your day; it is impossible!

Even if you wanted to be, it would be like walking on a bridge over the fire of hell. You would not be able to hold on for long, because that would not be your natural temperament. You would just be dressing up in a way of being that was not your own.

And even if you tried to be tough, no one would take you seriously. They would always see in you this mercy, this gentleness, this spiritual flow, this closeness... That is why people systematically come to you. They come to consult you, to take advice from you, to confide their secrets in you because you have this ability to receive them.

As for you, the brute, the corporal idol, you are the problem!

Break this *nafs*, split your heart, and, for the love, put forth and fan the *athar* of the *risâla*[4] of *sayiduna* al-Mustafa ﷺ. It is only then that the *risala* will reveal itself to you.

----

4   *Athar* of the *risala* means vestige of the message.

Burn in the fire of the love

Look for the support of Allâh to join Him. The door of Allâh does not have a guardian who is blocking the access. The door of Allâh is open for sincere people. In the Way, you learn the purification of the *nafs* from its passions which constitute the dimensions that belong to the *fana*. If you can shed it, then you will go through and you will reach the Goal. Reaching the Goal, is to simply burn and burn out completely.

You will burn then.

Al-Junayd (*radiAllâh 'anhu*) says that the one who will claim to have reached the Goal, in reality, has only reached *Saqar*[5]. Come in and burn your whole being in it, and get guidance from it.

Did not Musa (*'alayhi salam*) take the guidance from the fire? Did not he say: **I have perceived a fire; perhaps I can bring you a torch or find at the fire some guidance.**[6]

Therefore come into the fire of the ardent love and burn in it the entire dimensions that are not *fana*. In this way, you will be entirely guided. Bring us back a firebrand of the *athar* of the *risala* through which you will transmit to us the information emanating from the Tree. This tree from which the Lord manifesting Himself and from which the

....

5   The fourth degree of the Hell.
6   Surah Ta-Hâ, verse 10.

love was expressed. From that Tree, you saw a star of great brilliance through which you saw your Lord then exclaiming, **There is my Lord!**[7]

After that, you did not want anymore to be deprive of the vision of the star. If it came to disappear, you would reject at the same time all things that disappear. And if it came nearer, you would find in its proximity an infinite enlargement. Then you would love the nearness of the Lord and you would say: **This one is greater.**[8]

Thus, you would go from a world to another one, extinguishing the whole dimensions and staying in one and only one direction, a dimension without beginning or ending. Finally, you would exclaim: **I have turned my face towards the One who has originated the heavens and the earth—being upright—and I am not one of the polytheists.**[9]

Be careful here, we are not speaking about the One who created something from another thing (*khalaqa*), but about the One who brought the thing out of nothing (*fatara*). It means that when we refer to the Name al-Fatir[10], we are returning, in reality, to what there was before the appearance of matter, elements, and even the movement. We are returning to the state of primordial stillness (*sukoûn*) that means to the direction of the absolute, which you see precisely as described by the Prophet ﷺ:

....

7   Surah al-Anam, verse 76.
8   Surah al-Anam, verse 78.
9   Surah al-Anam, verse 79.
10   The Creator.

"Do you have difficulties to see the moon at night when it is full?" The companions answered: "No, ô Messenger of Allâh!" So, the Prophet ﷺ said: "Certainly, this is how you will see Him."[11]

Here, there is no traffic jam. Each one, whatever and wherever he is, whatever his spiritual station, whatever his state... because if we gather together in a group of people, we all see the sun and the moon when they rise in the sky. Nothing prevents us seeing them unless clouds shroud them. But no one can stop you from seeing the sun.

When are you divested of it?

It is when you do not make the effort to look up and see it. That is how you become veiled by your vision and your consideration of others—you start watching so-and-so. By this way, you are fussing with what is low (*sufli*) and neglecting what is high (*'olwi*). This is the cause of the disciple's distance from the Divine Presence.

Instead of taking care of the vision of the Lord's Light, of which you loudly claim to have taken the *bay'a*, this light that you received in one instant (*lamha*), but which you do not bother to contemplate. Rather, you are looking after what is low (*sufli*).

You are saying to yourself: "Ô this one outstrips me... I have to get back up to the front!" You start what you present as a competition for excellence whereas it is not. This competition is only desire, jealousy and hate. You became the servant of a spiritual degree and not the servant of the Lord who established this spiritual degree.

....

11 Al-Bukhariy and Muslim.

If you were linked to your Lord, you would not watch the one who is with you, you would not even consider him as existent. You would stay perpetually absent from all what you have around you.

The light and its usefulness

Because there are people who are wondering: "What is its usefulness, this Light?" It is rather you, what is your usefulness!?

The Light is the lantern of the *haqiqa* which permits you to perceive the deepest sense and the most banal elements of your daily life. From your children, your neighbours, to your job ... including the dirties tasks of the *dunia*! In other words, if you do not have the Light, you do not have the capacity to taste to the sense of the life in this world.

By this Light, what is in the domain of unknowable (*ghayb*) disclose to you and at least you understand what does "*ghayb*" means, because before receiving this Light, you heard a lot about the *ghayb*. You received a lot of information about this topic but without really realizing. It was just information you believed of course. We did not call your faith in the *ghayb* into question. However, you did not realize you did not have the *tahqiq* by the clear and concrete vision of what you have faith in.

After receiving the Light, you see this *ghayb* and you are able to make the difference and to distinguish what is darkness and what is Light. You access to the true Science, you achieve the Knowledge (*ma'rifa*) of Allâh, it means His Essence, His Attributes, His Laws and His Acts. If you do not have the Light, you cannot even achieve the realization of the adorations that brought us *sayiduna* al-Mustafa ﷺ and that you have to do.

You cannot also seize the sense of the *noubouwa*, of the *risâla*, of the revelation (*wahiy*) you cannot assert the difference between *noubouwa* and *risâla*. It is only by the Light, which is in your heart, that you will be able to understand the real sense of *noubouwa*. You will understand that, in fact, there is no difference from a message to another, that nothing was added or removed. But rather, each prophet and messenger brings us relative clarification of the Muhammadian entity who synthesises them and assembles everything within by the fact that he is the first and the last of all prophets ﷺ.

You will seize and you will understand the true sense of the revelation (*wahiy*). For common people, the revelation is a divine inspiration transmitted and expressed by the angel's tongue regarding the one whose God did a donation of this Light. He discovers to what the inspired revelation returns (*wahiy al-ilhâm*), to what the angel's revelation returns, to what shaytân's revelation returns, to what angels and devils' revelation returns. He also discovers how these last ones fight and harm humanity, how angels manifest themselves as prophets, how the revelation achieves them, how they access the knowledge of *malakoute* of heavens and earth. How all these elements are known?

By the light of Allâh! Not orally neither in writing!

Our Lord says Himself in the Quran **And thus did We show Abraham the *malakûte* of the heavens and the earth that he would be among the certain [in faith].**[12] Be careful, the verse does not speak about informing! It is written: **We show...**, it is really about the vision, the *mushâhada*, it is not written "We will teach to Abraham..." or something similar.

It is the same for the knowledge of the heart, that people named like a muscle, a pump which diffuses the blood in the body, and by the Light of Allâh, this heart becomes a *fou'âd*[13]. How could a muscle carry a Seigneurial Knowledge? This is not imaginable ... then how it can be possible?

You have to understand, this is an obligation for you, in accordance to the hadith *qudsi*: "*My heaven and My earth could not contain Me contrarily to the heart (qalb) of My faithful servant who could.*"[14] So you have to know what is the heart (*qalb*). Yet, the sense of the heart cannot be seized only by the Light of Lord ﷻ.

It means that all these definitions that you had in the past, you have to remove them outright in your head. It is not about denying words themselves but rather calling the sense that we give them into question.

You have to discover and understand how and to what extend the armies of angels and demons are facing themselves in your heart. The messenger of Allâh ﷺ tells us in a hadith: "*Shaytân circulates in the human being as blood circulates in the body, and I was afraid lest Shaytân might insert*

....

12   Surah al-Anam, verse 75.
13   The innermost.
14   Hadith *qudsi* reported by many sufis masters including al-Ghazali.

an evil thought in your minds."[15] No one denies this hadith ... but here, let's pay attention, what is the term "human being" referring to?

Whatever who you are, whatever your spiritual degree, you are and you remain a human—the Shaytân is circulating in you, through your veins! And in the hadith *qudsi* aforesaid, Allâh informs us that neither heavens nor the earth would be able to contain Him. Contrarily, to the heart of His believer servant that means that this heart understands the higher degrees, with angels. So you have to know how these two forces are opposing each other.

You have to know how you can distinguish the angelic insufflation from demoniac insufflation. You have to know the beyond, the Heaven, the Hell, the grave's punishment, the *sirat*, the balance, rendering of accounts. You have to understand and seize the sense of the vision of Allâh ﷻ and the contemplation of His Face. The common human denies, naturally, the reality of the contemplation of Allâh ﷻ despite what Lord says: **This day, there will be resplendent faces contemplating their Lord.**[16]

Some also deny the clear meaning of the hadith *sahih*: "According to Abu Hurayra (*radiAllâhu 'anhu*), people said: "*Ô Messenger of Allâh, will we see our Lord in the day of Resurrection?*"

The Prophet ﷺ *replied:*

— Do you have difficulties to see the sun when there is no cloud?

---

15 *Sahîh* al-Bukhâriy and Muslim.
16 Surah al-Qiyâma, verses 22 and 23.

— No, Ô Messenger of Allâh!

— Do you have difficulties to see the moon the night where it is full when there is no cloud?

— No, Ô Messenger of Allâh!

— Certainly, you will see Him at the Day of Resurrection like this."[17]

The Prophetic Word is really clear. At the moment where that was said, that means that you have a part in the Vision.

You will also have to know what is the divine Proximity, to know the gladness that the proximity of angels is procuring and the frequentation of prophets; to know the prevalence of some degrees regarding others in Heaven and so on; to know how these residents would see each of them.

How is this vision possible?

It is through the Star of great sheen (*al-kawkab ad-durriy*) that residents of Heaven can see each other like shining Stars. In this sense, the hadith is telling us clearly: *"My companions are like stars: whatever which one you are following, you will be well guided."*[18] That means that they are Stars and if they come to take place and live in the sky, they do so thanks to the Light of *sayiduna* al-Mustafa ﷺ.

This is what we designate in books like unveiling science (*'ilm al-moukâchafa*) and that is what we call the *kachf*. Be careful, the *kachf*, is not about knowing what a person is doing in his home when no one can see him. No, the *kachf* consists of knowing the Lord's Laws ﷻ in the nothingness that is the world where we are living. If you seize the divine Law which govern this nothingness, you will seize the

----

17   *Sahîh* al-Bukhâriy and Muslim.
18   Reported by ibn 'Abd al-Barr.

unveiling, you will seize the deep and esoteric sense. It is that which will be useful for you on the Last Day!

This day, it will be completely useless to know what this person did to this one, when no one saw him, or be able to read in people's heads. You will not be questioned on that! Rather, you will be questioned on this Law: did you show equity in your pathway, did you faithfully conform to the tracking of the prophet ﷺ?

The Messenger of Allâh ﷺ says in this sense in a hadith: "*This is the way of Allâh, so follow it and do not follow paths which deviate*". That is what you will be asked on the Day of Judgement. This is where you find the unveiling science, by which the veil is lifted so that the Creator's mark appears to you creeping in each thing, and so that you become a concrete witness.

The goal is to strengthen your faith, your certitude and your attachment to the religion or rather to the epitome of the religion, the spirit of the religion, the flavour of the religion. Then you will accomplish the prayer, the fast and all adorations by tasting each of them.

In the appearance, you will not do more or less than a simple muslim, but you will be superior to this normal person by the Science. It means when the true flavour of this adoration will unveil itself to you. And then, when the hour strikes to accomplish the prayer, you will stand up without laziness and nonchalance. It will not be a burden for you. Instead, it will be a source of Proximity and regrowth.

The light and a guide

When someone goes out into an obscure night, a black night, without any glow and walking on a rough path, he can fall or stumble. It is then that he needs the help of a lamp and a guide. The guide, knowing perfectly the way, is the only person able, and in a position, to bring you out of the forest and guide you in the city. Regarding the lamp, it is indispensable so that you can see where you put your feet. How is it possible to plan an entire life in this lowly world without the Light of the Prophet ﷺ!? How can we know if you are a part of Light's people or not?

It is very simple: take a place in an obscure piece and see if you are able to perceive things around you. You will soon realize that, obviously, you are blind. You lost the Light of the *haqiqa* which linked you and lead you to the Knowledge of the Creator, but on top of that, you do not even have a guide! Even if you have the Light, you will need a guide to teach you how to interact with this Light.

So, watch your state. You are blind and you need someone to help you, but when a person presents himself and proposes to take you by the hand, you answer him: "Leave me alone, you do not know anything. I am a *faqih*: I am a scholar, I have a great experience of the Way."

Ok then go. Let us see...

What experience of the Way do you have? How can you pretend when you have never been there?

The light is a distinction

Allâh guides whoever He wills to His light.[19] The Apparent by Himself, The One who makes appear others, guide to His contemplation and His Knowledge those He will want between His privileged beloveds.

It is here that you realize, truly, that the Lord loved you because if you did not have the Light, what would be your particularity?

Some people strut and pretend to be *majdhoub* or to be among people of the spiritual opening. However, if you do not have the Light, your state is no more and no less than those of the common people – you are exactly like them. Even if you had been educated to the highest levels of knowledge and understanding, without Light you have nothing more than anyone else.

These things are not enough to make you a privileged person, a person with a rare specialness that others do not have. They too, if they really wanted what you have, they would only have to act as you have acted, and they would achieve what you have achieved, or even more.

....

19   Surah an-Nur, verse 35.

However, this Light, they are unable to reach it, except if they abide by what was established by the Creator to reach it. When Allâh favours His beloved ones, He leads them to His contemplation and to His knowledge (*ma'rifa*).

As for you, who pretends to be a part of the privileged whereas you have no vision, no knowledge… you are far, very far! It is like if you mixed the Light with the darkness, it is not allowed. Come back to the righteousness instead of thinking and dwell on past things, things you have sacrificed time but have not benefited you in any way.

You imagine yourself being among righteousness people (*istiqama*). You have practiced the evocation of Allâh with such a fervour that you have filled your heart but this *dhikr* in which you have persisted for a long time, has never obtained any result, any sign, any of these luminous theophanies!

From there, you must realize that your work did not come to fruition. And regarding the words of the Imam Malik, you are even a *fasiq*[20]: you have memorized the Law, without looking for the spirit of the Law. You have memorized a science which is only on your tongue but if you open your heart, there is darkness…darkness… an absolutely terrifying state.

If something were to fall on it, we would see neither the beginning nor the end. This darkness is **Or [they are] like darkness within an unfathomable sea which is covered by waves, upon which are waves, over which are clouds— darkness, some of them upon others. When one puts out**

....

20 Pervert.

his hand [therein], he can hardly see it. And he to whom Allâh has not granted light - for him there is no light.[21]

This is the state of your heart: close your eyes and become aware of your state!

In the opposite, if you are one of the Light's people, the talents of the speakers do not matter very much. The correctness and accuracy of pronunciation in reading are not your priority because you base with certainty (*yaqin*) on a return to the Luminous Origin, in such a way that sometimes you are struck by this light, that you no longer see the slightest trace of existence of yourself, and that the Light has submerged everything. And so... you rejoice, you gloat because the Creator embraced all your presence.

How could you deny that? How could you continue to settle for appearances of a spoken science, quotes transmitted from the masters of our masters which thcy pronounce themself on the base of a Luminous certainty?

You took the appearance of words and you abandon the spirit. You have gathered information that you repeat with your tongue. You have begun to sing it and slip it here and there in your beautiful speeches. But you have forgotten the *haqiqa* of this speech, which is the truly spirit, Light, guidance and return to the Origin. This is what our Lord favoured His beloved ones with, like His prophets and His Saints.

The one who does not see this Light and who does not reach His knowledge, has no privilege, no particularity that would differentiate him from the rest of people. He belongs

....

21   Surah an-Nur, verse 40.

only to the common rights people. We do not say that he is among the misguided because his apparent acts are not those of the misguided but the works and the science as abundant they may be, as long as the veil remains, they are returned to nothing.

As long as the veil persists, whoever you are, we cannot consider you as a scholar and we cannot praise and elevate you as the holder of a science. As long as the veil persists, even if you were to stay up all your nights in prayer and fast all your days, we could not elevate you and praise you. Because, if your science and your work does not bring you any fruit... what is the interest? What good is it for you if, in spite of everything, you remain in a veil of darkness?

Do not be surprised to see the light

It is important to understand that the *bay'a* is not a simple handshake! No! At the moment you approach, at the moment you follow the Way and its principles—even from far—at the moment you have the certainty in the deep of your heart... you have the *bay'a*.

If the *bay'a* was just about the touch, hand in hand, people who are in far country would not be able to take it whether by phone or simply by taking the *wird tabarruk*...

Some people say: "I just took the *wird tabarruk* and now, I am seeing the Light...". Of course! It is not surprising that you are seeing the Light. What will be surprising for us it is that you cannot see it! In our *tariqa*, what is awkward, is not the fact that you are doing the *wird* and that you can see the Light. What will be shocking and abnormal, it is that you are doing the *wird* and you are not able to see anything! Yes, that would seem very strange to us.

If you are practicing our *wird* and you are able to see the Light, it is banal because the Tree is living! So, His *wird* is living too! However, if you are practicing the *wird* of another Shaykh or another *tariqa* and nevertheless this spiritual and esoteric flow does not reach you, then you have to know your *tariqa* is simply dead and your tree is dry and useless.

Now, if the Tree is living but you are not able to take anything from it, it is a problem linked to yourself and not to the Tree. If one hundred people come to take the *bay'a* and have seen the Light, then another has come but has not seen anything. The problem is coming from the person who did not see anything and not from the Tree.

But here we are, you refuse to admit that the problem is coming from you. You always return the guilt to others. How can you be able to learn, to educate your *mustaqarr*, to be able to receive this great news (*naba' al-'adhim*)? You are incapable because you are always torn by pride and vanity, you blame others for your faults and you are putting yourself in the bottom of the pyramid as if you are the embodiment of purity.

The Lord says though: **So do not claim yourselves to be pure; He is most knowing of who fears Him.**[22]

....

22 Surah an-Najm, verse 32.

To the one who doubts
the vision of his Lord

When the pre-eternal divine Beauty (*al-jamal*) appears, it is as the Beloved himself describes it in a way that cannot be more explicit: "*You will see your Lord on the Last Day like you are seeing the moon on a night where it is full; or like if you are seeing the sun when it is at its zenith and not covered by any cloud.*"[23]

From there, each of you have to meditate on this vision at the state of wakefulness (*mushahada*) which is occurring during the *dhikr*. "You will see your Lord on the Last Day..." once the individual dies, his Last Day (*qiyama*) appears, for him, whether his death is voluntary and initiatory or natural and inevitable.

"*... like you are seeing the moon on a night where it is full or like you are seeing the sun when it is at its zenith and that it is not covered by any cloud.*" So, it concerns the manifestation of the Beauty (*jamal*) of the Truth ﷻ.

As for what is Majesty (*jalal*), He ﷻ says: **No vision can encompass Him, but He encompasses all vision.**[24] Thus, when He is manifesting, gazes become included (*indarajat*) in His Face, which is nothing else except the absolute gaze

....

23 *Sunan* at-Tirmidhiy.
24 Surah al-Anam, verse 103.

(*al-basar al-mutlaq*), so that the one who is watching from a determinate angle (*muqayyad*), his lights will appear included (*indarajat*) in the pre-eternal light and he will not see anything else except Himself by Himself.

This is why, when al-Mustafa ﷺ was questioned—be careful, this hadith is sharping and irrevocable—all those who are doubting, all those who are deviating from the clear and obvious Truth, al-Mustafa ﷺ answers to you by this word which is in *Sahih Muslim*! Ô you, people of the doubt, open your ears well. Old and young, you are here a whole group of people who does not move forward straight.

Today, there is no longer "I know, I have a deep knowledge…". No. Bring us back the Quran and the Sunna and establish the irrefutable evidence on yourself and on others.

The messenger of Allâh ﷺ was interrogated: "*Have you seen your Lord?*" What was the answer? Look, enjoy the depth of his words, enjoy the sciences of eloquence and the perfect speech, his transmission of the entire message, clear and concise. He ﷺ replied: "*A light that I even see now.*" Be careful, he did not say: "I see Him into light". If you have a level in the Arabic language, you are aware of the rift that separates these two formulations.

"*A light that I even see now.*" That means: whether at my beginning, my middle or my end, I lost my corporeal nature, in a definitive and absolute way, and then saw an exhaustive light.

Only His light is and remains; exalted be His transcendence. So, from there, what will you be able to imagine… How do you think that you will see your Lord, ô you the great knower, ô you who did the *khalwa* and who is among people of *dhikr*? How do you think you will see your Lord?

The Messenger of Allâh ﷺ explains you: "*A light that I see even now*" and you, you afford to denigrate the light. You come and you talk to me about visual impairment or a reflection infused in your eye... *subhanAllâh*! Would it be possible to Man to see Him another way than this one? No my dear... this is the Way of the Beloved ﷺ: "*A light that I even see now.*"

The default is not in the light but more in your black and murky heart. The darkness stacked on top of each other and covering you entirely, to the point where even when you move your hand, the hand of the spiritual aspiration (*irada*), it does not take much and you may not see anything of the attributes of Allâh.

If you are not able to perceive the attribute, how can you perceive the pre-eternal essence?

The default is not in the *shari'a* but rather in the one who heard the *shari'a* and stuck to the stupidity of his intellect, without ever understanding anything. This is the true issue.

Al-Mustafa ﷺ expressed this, namely the inclusion (*indiraj*) of all lights in the *haqiqa* of this ultimate and supreme light so that there remains neither looking nor looked. His nature of mountain was completely pulverized, it means his corporeality and only **Allâh, light of the heavens and the earth**[25] remains.

Allâh says to Musa (*'alayhi salâm*): **You will not see me.**[26] Then, when He manifested to the mountain of Musa, Musa was pulverized in the *haqiqa* of Musa. He fainted and when he woke up, he exclaimed: **Exalted are You!** He outstripped

....

25 Surah an-Nur, verse 35.
26 Surah al-A'râf, verse 143.

the station (*maqam*) of the exclusivity (*ahadiya*) then his duality was included (*indarajat*) in the exclusivity of the True ﷻ and he exclaimed: **Exalted are You! I have repented to You, and I am the first of the believers.**[27]

This is the Quran you cannot change it. Spare us your *tafsir* who is going in the direction of your passions. Take the verse as it is: **I have repented to You and I am the first of the believers.** Like if there had never been any believer before him.

I am the first of the believers is to distinguish from "I am a believer among the believers".

The question is to know if you too reached this state where all your being is pulverized and where you become among the precursors of the station of *al-imân*.

I am the first of the believers means he ignored all people who came before and he included all of them in the *hadra* of the absolute and pre-eternal light. And then, he expressed and revealed the beginning of the attribute's apparition (*sifa*) of the True ﷻ or if he wanted to say to you, in others terms, that by Musa, the True is manifesting. **I am the first of the believers** or there is no one except me. Me and I alone. I am the one who knew you ô Lord!

That is all. Musa (*'alayhi salâm*) is challenging you through this Quranic verse.

Go remove it from the Quran, ô you who criticize the Way of Allâh, ô you who accomplished the *dhikr* and the *khalwa* but who is, today, riddled with the doubt! We already said it last week and we repeat it today and we will repeat it as long as we will be in the *hadra* of *lam*: all those

....

27   *Ibid.*

who have even an atom of doubt, it is better for them to stop coming here. Even though we will have only four people in this weekly sitting.

What a shame, after three years or even five years of *tariqa*, and we are here barking without respite. Sometimes a verse of the Quran, sometimes a hadith and you are still here telling us: "No but Sidi Shaykh, I still have doubts...". Understand that you are Iblis walking on two feet. You have believed neither in what Allâh says nor in what al-Mustafa ﷺ says.

Fade away in the light

Allâh said: **Has there come upon man a period of time when he was not a thing [even] mentioned?**[28]

However, the time (ad-Dahr), is Allâh in accordance with the prophetic hadith: *"Let no one of you insult the time (ad-Dahr) because Allâh is the time."*[29]

Concerning the time period or the moment, it is a theophany between His theophanies throughout which Man has no existence. During all the period of this theophany, the servant has no existence: neither self-existence, nor existence by knowledge. Then he is a thing neither mentionable, nor nameable.

The person sits and begins to evoke the Beloved ﷺ. He begins by obtaining from him the approval (*idhn*) through which he will enter in the Presence of the Lord Almighty. And once the True is manifesting in him by the supreme beauty of His theophany, then effectively, the servant is not anymore even a mentionable thing. Neither by any characteristic, nor by a science, nor by anything else.

Because the verse is clear: **Has there come upon man a period (*hîn*) of time (*dahr*)...** meaning a manifestation among the manifestations of the True ﷺ.

....

28   Surah al-Insan, verse 1.
29   *Sahih* Muslim.

So, did a divine manifestation come to Man, whether it is a manifestation of His attributes or of His Names, so that he realizes the erasure and the total annihilation as *sayiduna* Musa (*'alayhi salam*) when a time period of the True reaches him and he disappears, along with the mountain which was in front of his eyes.

It is why *sayiduna* al-Mustafa ﷺ informs us in a hadith: "*I have a time in which I have no consideration (la yasa'uni) for anyone except my Lord.*"[30] There is a moment, a time period during which theophanies or manifestations of True appear to me. During this moment, this corporal envelope named Muhammad Ibn 'Abdillah is absolutely no longer existent and then, I am living through the manifestation of the True, meaning in His contemplation. This is the flavour of the *ma'rifa*.

It is not a matter of sticking to the theophany itself. No! Rather, understand what does it mean this theophany which has manifested to you, understand what it has done to you.

Sayiduna al-Mustafa ﷺ speaks to us about an hour that means a period during which he is fully and exclusively committed to the theophany or to the manifestation of your Lord. And when this moment begins, appear the detailed characteristics of *sayiduna* Muhammad ﷺ.

When do these characteristics of *sayiduna* al-Mustafa ﷺ appear?

They do not appear through you own knowledge of him, for example in his day-to-day life, on the pretext that you have read his biography or something similar. Rather, the characteristics of *sayiduna* al-Mustafa ﷺ appear during this

....

30   Hadith mentioned by al-Quchayriy in his *risâla*.

time in which he gives no consideration to anyone except his Lord. It is at this particular moment that the *haqiqa* of *sayiduna* al-Mustafa ﷺ appears; In the mirror of his Lord, so that he does not see no one except Himself ﷻ.

From there, you understand that the real knower (*'arif*) is in a time in which he has no consideration for anyone except his Lord. If at the same time, he stood in front of a mirror and looked into it, he would not see himself. He would see and would consider himself as completely erased, disappeared, without the slightest shred of existence.

The light will avoid you
the punishment of Allâh

This prophetic light, muhammadian and ahmadian ﷺ, does not manifest in any of Allâh's creatures without providing protection from His punishment. When the Lord ﷻ manifests to the disciple, that is through His light, in the heart of that disciple, obviously provided that the person respects, magnifies and sanctifies this light. He has to know that Allâh's punishment will not afflict him. The proof of this is explicit: **But Allâh would not punish them while you are among them.**[31]

If the space-time considerations have overwhelmed you at the point of altering your understanding of this clear verse, then go back to the time of al-Mustafa ﷺ if you want to shelter from divine punishment. In fact, the messenger of Allâh ﷺ is with you through His Luminous nature. He is Light. He is the enlightened torch. And because He is spreading over in you, it is unthinkable that Allâh punishes you.

Obviously, you like that. You like to be protected from the punishment. You like the *jamâl*. You do not like the knowledge (*ma'rifa*) more than you like the heavens. This is the truth.

....

31 Surah al-Anfal, verse 33.

Allâh ﷻ declares: **Allâh would not punish them while you are among them.** This is clear because as reported, this prophetic Light is the first of the creatures. He ﷺ says then: *"Lord, make me intercede for all those in whom You have placed me"* to which his Lord replied: **I have certainly granted you this, even before I created you.** In fact, the Lord only granted certain privileged people to receive His light, so that they would beg Him to spare them the punishment.

Furthermore, the Messenger of Allâh ﷺ informs:
"Allâh created the creation in the darkness then He projected in them His Light so that the one who is touched by this light is well-guided while the one who does not have it is lost."

This hadith is authentic (*sahih*) and plus, al-Albani certified it as authentic.

"Allâh created the creation in the darkness" that means in the nil (*'adam*), in the ignorance (*jahl*), deprived of all knowledge (*ma'rifa*). *"Then..."* according to another version *"He sprayed (rachcha)"* and in another version *"He projected (alqa) in them the Light so that the one who is touched by this light is well-guided."*

You want the guidance? In this case, look for the light of Allâh. If this light finds you, then you are effectively in the right guidance. In the opposite, if the light does not find you then you will never have anything except ignorance and darkness.

As for you, you are nothing (*'adam*) and you remain nothing. If the light reaches you or escapes you, your condition will not change. However, your attachment to the light, through its vision, is an attachment to the science (*'ilm*) and to the deep knowledge (*ma'rifa*), in addition to an attachment to the salvation and the divine protection.

Al-Tabarâniy reported that the Messenger of Allâh ﷺ says: "*Allâh will resuscitate the servants on the Last Day and will address to the scholars among them…*". Be careful, always, when you hear about the scholars, it is not about those that we consider today and who are just people who memorize. Al-Shâfi'iy says: "*The science is a Light and the Light of Allâh is not given to the sinner.*"

Allâh will resuscitate the servants on the Last Day and will address the scholars among them: "*Ô scholars, I certainly haven't placed in you the science ('ilm) to punish you after. So, go away because I have forgiven you.*" In other words: "I certainly have not placed in you the light to punish you after. Rather, I have placed in you to forgive you, to receive your repentance."

Regarding the differences
between the visions of disciples

The role of the Shaykh is to purify the *nafs*. The cure of this *nafs* is to permit it to return to its origin, to permit it to return where it comes from, that means the world of the absolute purity (*'alam al-safa*). In fact, the *nafs* is a subtle and unstable body. Thus, when it was melded into the physical world, it turned towards a physical form too and then was filled by the darkness. Henceforth, it needed to be purified from this physical trouble which affected it.

But the *nafs* cannot be purified only if it is melded into the purity. As well as it changed by the mixing of trouble (the physical trouble), it can only change again and return to its original state by being mixed again with purity, and thus become a pure *nafs*, or spirit (*rûh*). The *nafs* is feminine not masculine. And it is through the marriage that the feminine can beget. So, it is imperative for the *nafs* to get married to a purified spirit in order to beget the fruit of the esoteric knowledge (*ma'rifa*). That the *nafs* come to the Goal lonely and beget anything by itself is obviously impossible.

To give an example regarding the *nafs*, it is like a piece of coal. If we take a piece of coal and we clean it with water, with cleaning product, is it going to become a white piece?

Of course not. Scrape it, pumice it, throw it in the sea if you want, the piece of coal will remain a piece of coal. Like the *nafs*.

The truth is that the case of the *nafs* is simple: You need to expose her to an essence (*iksir*) which is superior to it, namely the fire. The fire and the coal get married, they mix together and how does the piece of coal become when it is placed in the fire? Its colour changes. It becomes red, white, green, blue, it gives you all the colours of the *michkat*[32]. It is the same for the *nafs*.

If you imagine that through the *dhikr* you will do by yourself meaning by your own personal efforts or by the lecture of sufi's books, you will achieve something... So, you say "me, I do the *dhikr*, I do this and I do that... in order to purify my spirit...". Do whatever you want, for as long as you want, in vain, you will only try to clean the piece of coal by dipping it in the water. You will put it into bleach, detergent, you will brush it but the coal will remain a coal. Even if you brush it all day long.

It is the same for the *nafs*. Except if you married her to the one whose elixir (*iksir*) is stronger than yours, someone whose the strength is more important than yours, someone whose subtlety exceeds yours, because in this case, your *nafs* will be able to give the fruit of this marriage, meaning the secret of the knowledge of the uncreated essence (*al-dhât al-azaliya*).

So, go back to your state and ask yourself this question: are you among those who accept this marriage? The answer is no. You are always looking for the loneliness and the

....

32 Recess.

Shaykh, you think he is a statue, a stone, an idol: "Sidi Shaykh, make me *du'a*...", "Sidi Shaykh, I will have my exams soon, make me *du'a* for my success", "Sidi Shaykh, I am getting married... make me *du'a* so that my wife to be pious", "Sidi Shaykh, my wife is pregnant, make me *du'a* so that the baby is healthy." The Shaykh is a statue to who your order invocations.

However, "Sidi Shaykh, how should I do the *dhikr*? How can I contemplate the light? How can I reach the knowledge?" Deleted. That, it does not even come to your mind. From the *fuqara*, there is only requests for invocations: "Make me *du'a* for me, I am sick, I need this, I need that... I want money, I want to get married..."

You have the certitude that the Shaykh can help you to obtain, but you do not have the certitude that if the Shaykh helps you to know your Lord, it is better for you? Rather than asking your Shaykh to invoke for you, why do not you prefer to invoke yourself for yourself? No, you do not have time for that.

So here we are, we are taking our time to invoke for yourself: "O you... may the Lord gives you what you want..." The invocation is done and worked effectively. But it never touches you. Simply because you are not ready to receive it (*talaqqiy*). You are at the opposite of the wave. The light is blazing. It is like if the sun has risen and lit the whole world, while you are in a closed room where you have taken care to close all the shutters.

How will this sun penetrate in your home? Where will its rays go?

The sun has risen, you have closed the windows, the shutters and you have drawn the curtains over them. The people outside are all at work, all enjoying the sun but you, you did not even see it! Why? It is not because it did not rise, no, because then, no one would be able to testify it. So why does this person see the full moon, why does this person see the divine names (*al-asma'*), why is this person in the Prophet's presence, while nothing has reached you yet? Why?

Simply because you closed and locked the house of your heart. You closed it and even caulked it. So much so that when you talk with the Shaykh, you show the most total state of hypocrisy: "Sidi Shaykh, you are in my heart... Sidi Shaykh, I love you..." whereas, if you had a bomb, you would have exploded it in my hands.

So, tell me, where will this light be able to come from?

Think about it. When we come to take the *bay'a* of the Shaykh, there is one who sees the sun, another who sees the moon, another who sees the star and another, the Shaykh has to repeat it five or even seven times before he sees something. Why?

Why, one sees the sun, the other sees the moon? Would the Shaykh have deceived them? Would he have given to some and divested others? No. It is always the same verse he uses to transmit the *bay'a*, for everybody, men and women. The same *du'a,* the same strength, the same energy, the same state of presence, the same state of erasure of all spatial consideration, the same state of persistence by Allâh so that the verse would be perfectly established: **Surely those who pledge allegiance to you are actually pledging allegiance to Allâh.** It is up to the Shaykh to erase himself, as well as the disciple, so that only Allâh remains. **Allâh's Hand is over theirs**, He establishes the presence of all the divine names, which testify about this pact and from then: **Whoever breaks their pledge, it will only be to their own loss. And whoever fulfils their pledge to Allâh, He will grant them a great reward.**[33] that means once the Shaykh will tell him "Look", instantaneously he will see the sun, another will instantaneously see the moon.

So why does this person see the sun, this person sees the moon and this person, when the Shaykh tells him "Look", he answers: "Where? I cannot see nothing!?" Because the disciple is not in the mood to receive (*talaqqiy*) that suit. Concerning the Shaykh, he is sending all the energy without any distinction between each others. If the wayfarer does not receive anything, it is due to the doubts in his heart, due to his distance and due to the hate which overwhelms him. Even if he shakes his tongue to express the opposite and repeats "I love you, I love you..." there is no love in reality.

The true love is the Light. When you see the Light, you do not need to tell the Shaykh "Me, I love you." The Shaykh knows how to distinguish his beloved ones and his enemies.

When you went in the *khalwa*, you completely revealed who you were, from the moment your mother gave birth to you until the ultimate Meet, if you are among them though. In the *khalwa*, you revealed if you were among people of Heavens or people of Hell. In the *khalwa*, your reality became as clear as black writing on a white sheet for the Shaykh.

....

33 Surah al-Fath, verse 10.

May the frequentation
of the disciples does not harm you...

We keep telling you not to worry about others in your pathway. Stay focused on yourself. Why? Because what matters to you is your folder. You need to have all your papers in order. It does not matter if so-and-so is remaining on line or not. To each his own business. What matters is that I am remaining on line. I have to get my visa, my identity card... everyone should take care of themselves. If you had been mindful about your personal state, you would have forgotten those who are with you.

So how is the Shaykh essential to you here?

Simply because he helps you to be in order with your papers. He tells you what kind of paper you are missing, that you need an identity picture and so on. And that is why you have to show *adab* to him and to apply what he asks you, because it is he who knows what is missing in your folder.

But you, by going to talk with so-and-so, to look for advice alongside someone else, you become confused. Because you do not talk to the right office... Each one has his own intention. One is here for the work, one for the marriage, one for the studying and you for example, who is here to learn, you go and you talk to the one who is looking for a wife. Understandably, he will tell you that you have to get married and that you need a certificate of celibacy and so on. So please understand...

You have to understand that the *murid* is absolutely useless for the *murid*. When you stay during hours and hours with the disciple talking, you have to know finally, you turn him off and he turns you off. And know that this intention that you have initially in your heart, he ends up modifying you and introducing something else. You come maybe for science and this other person you are talking; he is looking for something else. He is talking to you depending on the intention he has in his heart and his intention ends up affecting you, and you, in surprise, want to do like the others.

You end up following this person and you reach this hidden goal in the heart of the one that you are listening to. If it was a goal about the *dunia*, you would reach it effectively. And if it was a goal concerning an application in the practice of the *dhikr*, you would reach it too but you will not have anything more!

It is why *moulay* 'Abdessalâm ibn Machîch explains: "The one who is leading you to *dunia*, has certainly deceived you..." and the *murid* with the *murid*, that is what it leads you. You must not bury your head in the sand. Regarding the one who thinks he is superior, the one who thinks he has understood everything, in the best case, he can only lead to the *awrad* (*dhikr*).

"The one who leads you to the *awrad* has certainly tired you..." But the Shaykh, no. The Shaykh leads you directly to Allâh! "Regarding the one who leads you to Allâh, he has certainly given you the good advice".

That is why the Shaykh speaks in front of everybody. Because, he knows that there is no one except Allâh. The *murid*, no. He cannot talk in front of everybody. He has to isolate you and put you aside to avoid being heard by others because he is full of darkness. He needs the darkness to talk with you. The Shaykh, no. He pours everything on you in the midst of the sitting. Take or leave what he is giving you, when he is giving it to you, it is your problem. The other, no. The other, he is shaping you "Come, we go and get a coffee...". He proposes you a coffee to better turn your brain. He calls you on the phone, he sends you messages and asks you to discuss with him "Come and discuss, we help each other..." You will help each other until you realize that your heart has been turned. And this heart, if the Shaykh had not opened it, you will remain completely blind, you do not even know where to place your foot. So beware, be careful...

This opening of the heart's vision (*basira*), we give it to you as of the *bay'a*. Why the *murid*—whatever who he is—cannot open this *basira* yet we can? Because we lead people to Allâh! And he, if he cannot open it, leads you only to futile things. He will lead your heart into turmoil. You must imagine he is opening your heart, he will fill it with sand. And for you, it is exactly the same thing! When you see the *murid* imagining that you will open his heart, in fact, you are just adding issues to those he already has! You are filling his eyes with sand until he is unable to see anything.

You cannot take two imams at the same time for the same prayer, it is not possible, you have to then choose carefully your imam!

The Messenger of Allâh ﷺ explains: "*Your imams are your intercessors towards Allâh: if you want to purify your prayer, take as your imam the best among you.*" And who is this one who will intercede for you? It is this one who will lead you to the Presence of al-Mustafa ﷺ. It is the imam whose the *hijra* has been for Allâh and His messenger ﷺ. You are following so-and-so... why? Because he has a 4x4? Because you like how he talks? Because you like his culture?

Be careful!

Be careful about your intention... it is not him who is bad! He is doing what he has to do. It is rather you; it is your intention which is bad! Because you are following it with a specific goal, you have an interest and for this reason, you have to know that you will not win neither in this world nor hereafter.

The war against the carelessness

We say that Abou Bakr Al-Chibliy—in the beginning of his pathway—used to keep with him a little bundle of branches. Every time he forgot the *dhikr*, he hit himself with one of them until it broke. And the bundle depleted each day before the night.

But why did he do that? Why did he torture himself like that? Simply because he was afraid to fall into the carelessness (*ghafla*)! Every time he became aware of his carelessness, he was hitting himself.

But, be careful, his state of carelessness, here, was not a reference to the absence of *dhikr*, no! Rather, it is about inattention and neglect of propriety's conditions who should accompanied the *dhikr*! Because obviously *sayiduna* Abu Bakr Al-Chibliy was among constant evocative people.

Thus, what should we say about the one who takes his *subha* and does his *dhikr* thinking about his wife? Even worse, there are people who are doing their *dhikr* thinking about sin! Here we are evoking a particular case.

What a shame... we introduce ourself as people who have made the *khalwa*, people who contemplate the Light of Lord and despite that, I have to sit and take time to remind the importance of the *dhikr*, the great benefit of its practice. These are things that we have to say to the common people! It is a topic that we use to do the *da'wa* in the market. For those who let themselves be submerged by the business and do not practice the *dhikr*. Here all of you are practising the *dhikr*, all of you did the *khalwa*. However, some of you lost and abandoned the conditions and the imperatives of the *dhikr*. It is for this reason that we have to do this reminder, to tune up. So no, we do not practice the *dhikr* when and how we want, whatever the position or the situation, whether you are busy or not.

You who love to quote Al-Hallâj, have a look at how Al-Hallâj was. He was doing the *ghusl* before each prayer! As for you, you do the *tayammum*. This is the difference between you and him. And if we ask you why did you do the *tayammum*, you reply that you are afraid to wet yourself with cold water. Al-Hallâj, was doing the *ghusl* with cold water before each prayer! This is the difference.

You did not do a sin and Al-Hallâj did not do a sin. But because he gave the importance to the prayer, he preceded it by the major ablution, accomplishing systematically the *ghusl* to purify himself from the state of *janâba* which is the carelessness, to purify himself from the consideration of things outside the divine, to purify himself from all thoughts which won his mind. It is by this way he proceeds in order to establish at best the link with his Lord. And each one differs, each one according to the force that the Lord bestowed to him in this sense.

To come back to the example of Al-Chibliy, who hit himself with branches when he was in the carelessness, when he had no branches left and he still continued to be won over by the carelessness, he hit his hands and his feet against the wall.

Here, we can say that it is like there was an exaggeration in the corporal punishment he imposed to himself... when we are aware about these narratives, we considerate that, really, it is exaggerated, it is too much, it is going too far but if we report these facts, it is to let you understand a thing. You have to be aware of how Allâh's people were used to deal with the carelessness. They are doing literally the war. It was a true war, a hard fight, body and soul.

Do not take this lightly! Read these narratives about these persons and realize the efforts that each of them did against their *nafs*.

This is where you would aspire to reach something exceptional of course, where you would like to transcend limits because if you want to continue to tell yourself: "it is ok, I prayed two *rak'at* ... I did one hundred prayers on the Prophet ... I did a ransom (*fidya*) of one hundred *istighfar*..." everybody do that!

See what people of Allâh are did to tame their *nafs* and avoid them being taken by the carelessness or affine their ability to focus or to meditate See what they did to always be focused on this secret that Allâh gave them. Their inside was a secret, their vision was light, their thoughts were science and their pathway was propriety (*adab*).

This is, truly, the one we call "*dhâkir*", the one who practises the *dhikr*.

Your efforts to purify
your *nafs* are useless...

The *nafs* cannot be purified on its own by the effort that the person is doing on herself. If the wayfarer thinks that he is able to purify his *nafs* without the companionship (*subha*), if he thinks that by this way, overnight, he could become a pure person, it is an obvious mistake. Because our Lord ﷻ informs us: **Do not self-purify yourself**[34] and in another verse: **It is Allâh who purifies who He wants.**[35]

How to purify this *nafs*?

Firstly, you are absolutely incapable of purify your *nafs* by yourself. It is Allâh who purifies the *nafs*. And the Lord did not say "Al-Rahman purifies who He wants" or "Al Sami' purifies who He wants". It is important because it means that if you want to pretend to this purification, you have to come back to the divine Name "Allâh".

If you think that you can achieve something of this purification of the *nafs* whereas you are and you remain perfectly ignorant about the Name indicator of the Essence... you are mistaken.

....

34 Surah an-Najm, verse 32.
35 Surah an-Nisa, verse 49.

When you hear "It is Allâh who purifies who He wants", leave the verse as it is, without adding or modifying His meaning. Here, it is the name "Allâh" who has been employed and not another one.

However, about the first verse which came on Al-Mustafa ﷺ, He did not say: "Read, by the name of Allâh" but **Read, by the name of your Lord (*rabbik*).**[36]

The subtlety of this indication is in the fact that the divine Name "al-Rabb"—the Lord—implies the necessity of the servant. Indeed, if there was no servant, the Lord could not be a Lord. Likewise, if there was no Lord, the servant could not be a servant. Regarding the ultimate Name "Allâh", "Allâh was while nothing was with Him and He is now how He always has been."[37]

If he had said: "It is the Lord (al-Rabb) who purifies who He wants" then you would be able to work on your own for your own purification. But here, **it is Allâh who purifies who He wants**, you cannot do anything on your own. Rather, you have to go back to the Ultimate Name.

Also, regarding the name "Allâh", we say we enter on it by his *hâ*. What does it mean?

It means that you have to fade away (*fanâ*) in his *fanâ*. If you achieve this extinction by doing the complete and absolute abstraction of yourself, then your *nafs* will not have an iota of existence. At this moment, there is good news for you: you come in … be careful, we do not say that you reach the purification! Rather, we say that you come in or you access the Name.

....

36 Surah al-'Alaq, verse 1.
37 *Iqâdh al-himam fi charh al-hikam*, Ibn 'Ajiba.

When can we consider that your *nafs* has been purified?

When you have known the different degrees of the Name who reunites all of them: Allâh, the indicator of the Essence.

And how could you reach the knowledge of this Name? For that, you have to look for the intermediary between you and Him (*wasitâ*). You need a good companion. You have to look for, not the one who will purify you, but the one who will teach you the divine Name because it is by your learning of the Name that the Lord will purify you.

Also, do not think that by sitting alone, by giving your time to the *dhikr* and adorations accordingly, that what your *nafs* tell you, will mean you obtain something. No, quite the reverse.

In this case, your adorations will become a veil for you. You will never access any deep knowledge and even worse, your deeds will become an obstacle which will veil you from the knowledge including your own *nafs*!

If you are one of those who have read books and have studied in university, you are going to formulate things that show that you did not live beside a living Shaykh. In this way, you have to know that you are completely unable to access the knowledge of the Name. How many people tried to come in by this door to finally descend into the misguidance?

Before to access the knowledge of the Name, it is necessary and essential for the person to have a look at his heart and to see that there is only darkness. You have to see and access the certitude that you are only darkness because if you think that you are *masha Allâh*, at this moment, you pretend indirectly to this state of purity (*tazkiya*) and you exempt yourself from the necessity to have a Shaykh. On the contrary, when the person recognizes to be only darkness, when the person admits his state of estrangement which is his, then he will be able to look for someone who can save him.

How should he do it? He has to go back to Allâh, beg The Almighty and then the Lord will guide him, through the one who will lead him to His knowledge.

Ô you who imagine you
can move alone in the way

You have to know, in the Way of the Light, only people who are worthy persevere. Take the light, come on. The Shaykh gives it to all those who ask for it but you have to know that sooner or later, only the true people of the Light will remain in this Way. As for the one whose truth is darkness, even if you discharge on him the entire light, he will always run away and go back to his darkness.

In this Way, only true people of the light persevere and this is thanks to the companionship (*subha*). We always remember that the companionship is the condition sine qua non.

Yes, because there are some people who take the light, then they affirm: "Me, I am going to work and make effort by my own, on my side. Disciples are bad. Disciples are hypocritical. This one is a thief. This one is always lying. And this one, he is not serious in his adorations".

As soon as you see things like that, you have to know that you are the liar. You are the one who is not serious in your adorations and you are the traitor! If you had been truly someone luminous, you would never have seen anything else but the light. As long as you see faults, it is only your faults. There is only your mirror that you see your own image.

It is why I say at the end, in this Way of the Light, only persevere the true people of the light and no one can continue in this way without the companionship (*subha*). Because the person who is alone and isolated, even if all secrets of the unknowable (*ghayb*) were revealed to him, so much so that he will begin to discover the thoughts of people around him or he will speak about what happen currently in Mecca by sitting here, you have to know that nothing good can ever come from him until he has accompanied a Shaykh. If he is alone, do not think that anything good can come from him. He can see whatever he wants, without the Shaykh, he cannot classify what he sees. He is completely unable to determine where he is or where he is heading.

Some people affirmed that "the one who has not a Shaykh, the Shaytân is his Shaykh."[38]

The wayfarer of this knowledge must not ever imagine he is able to reach it thanks to himself, by reading books of Sufi masters then by doing spirituals exercises on its own initiative. By Allâh, without a Shaykh, despite all the efforts that he can do, he will never succeed (*wusûl*).

Last week, there was a person to whom we have transmitted the secret of Lord. What did he imagine? He says: "I am in the *fasl*, I am in the scission, I have to isolate myself because it is like that when we are in the *fasl*". In other words, according to him, pursuant to the *fasl*, that is it, he does not need the Shaykh anymore. He isolates himself and the spiritual flows and the understandings will reach him.

....

38   *Words of the Shaykh* Abu Yazid al-Bistami.

I left him like that, in this state, for four years until he reached at the deepest degrees of the bewilderment. And then, I sent him a message. A simple message, two words, no more, if he heard them, he would wake up instantly. Then regrets would prey on him and burn him on the inside and he would learn a lesson like he never had before. He would understand in an instant that four years of efforts, four years of search in books, four years of *khalwa*, all that for a final note of 0 / 1000. Even by taking the Quran and by reading it from morning to night ... nothing. He will never reach nothing.

This is the importance of the Shaykh with disciples.

You imagine, ô you who declare: "The Shaykh gave me the secret ... the Shaykh gave me the light ..." you think that thanks to that, you succeeded, you won. No, whatever happens, whatever the situation, the Shaykh is smarter than you, he always has one step ahead. He lets you see the thing then he lets you work. His eyes follow you and notice what you accomplished. If what you do is in agreement with his follow-up then the understandings and the deeper senses will gush for you instantly.

But if you begin to take your own superficial thoughts as your deeper understandings or if you are falling back on lectures to move and progress ... even if "the Shaykh does not know anything", what he received, he received it from his own Shaykh and they are secrets of the Lord. It is he who is the key holder, this is what the Lord decided. Period. And these keys like for example the first secret, go on, providing all the efforts that you want. At the end, it is him who comes to you, he assembles all in a split second and he says to you "take, here is the secret of the *hâ*". Then, continue providing more effort, if you want, he will finish by coming to you, establishing a center (*markaz*) to this *hâ* and he will say to you, "This is the *lâm al-qabd*". Continue providing all the efforts of the world and in one night, he will spray you in the *markaz* and will say, "This is the *lâm al-ma'rifa*". Take up again, it is him again who will isolate you (*fasl*) from the entire universe while leaving you in him and you will imagine being separate from him. You will exclaim: "This is it, I am self-sufficient in my own spiritual dimension (*hadra*)". When, you remember that, you will realize how stupid you are.

And it is like that for all the secrets, so that you know that all the unveilings (*kachf*) which reached you, were not received by your own work. This light that you received, she does not appear out of the air, it is not a pure chance, it is coming from the follow up of a Shaykh. And what you receive is only up to your follow up. The more you conform to the Shaykh, the more you receive. This is clear and obvious for each of you. Those who are present receive. Regarding those who are present with their body but whose the spirit is elsewhere, they have to know that the light too, she escapes them.

The wayfarer can imagine that he is in the path of the serious, the path of the strictest righteousness whereas he turned his back on what he thinks he is moving towards. The disciple imagines being in front of the *qibla* whereas the *qibla*, he left it behind him and all the efforts he is doing to be closer to her only pushes her further away.

Know that the shaytân of this *tariqa* is a fine connoisseur. He is a specialist. He is a shaykh, in these things. He knows all the secrets. Do not think that you are better than him.

Allâh created Adam with His own hand while you are here only by the intermediary of a father and a mother. Adam (*'alayhi salâm*), He created him with His hand. You learnt divine names (*al-asma'*) by the intermediary of the Shaykh whereas him, the Lord Himself taught him: **He taught Adam the names of all things.**[39]

The Lord breathed His Spirit in him: **He fashioned them and had a spirit of His Own creation breathed into them.**[40] while for you, it is the angels who came to breathe into you your spirit whereas you were in your mother's womb in the fourth month.

In other words, your level, in comparison to Adam's level... it is worthless. Adam (*'alayhi salam*), Allâh created him with His own Hand, He breathed His Spirit in him. He taught him all the divine names, He made the universe bow down in front of him. The most distinguished between angels bowed down in front of Adam (*'alayhi salam*)...

What is the reality of your state in comparison to Adam (*'alayhi salam*)? Even so, Iblis pushed him to fail. Despite all degrees of distinguishment which are his ... Iblis succeeded to make him fall of his station (*maqam*) and he brought it down to the lowest possible until the earth, it means until his first physical form. Did you reach to that?

Just one letter, I have been teaching the *hâ'* for eight years, and you still did not get it. As for Adam (*'alayhi salam*), he realized all the names! The apparent and the hidden names with all their lectures.

....

39 Surah al-Baqarah, verse 31.
40 Surah as-Sajda, verse 9.

The insufflation of the spirit, you do not even know how to differentiate the spirit (*rûh*) from the *nafs*, you have no idea what is the descent (*tanazzul*) of the spirit in the *nafs* or in the intellect (*'aql*), you do not know anything about that, absolutely nothing. And if you pretend to have a particular knowledge, I am still alive, so come and tell me about your knowledge. You have no knowledge neither the spirit nor the divine name. You were not created in an immaculate purity body as Adam (*'alayhi salam*) but despite everything, you pretend infallibility. You assure "No, me all alone, on my side, I will do that and I will do this ..."

Then come, sit on your side and produce something. Show us.

Do not forget your past behavior

Let's take the example of prophets (*'alayhim salam*), those whose goal was truly the quest of Allâh's knowledge. Firstly, they never committed any sins. Their one and only aspiration was always, what would lead them through this knowledge. When they reached forty years, or before for some of them, their quest of Allâh's knowledge took shape and for them, it was not about shedding their sins and their bad habits they'd adopted many years before (like the *murid*).

When the *murid* comes here, in the beginning, he is carrying mountains of sin … let's be honest. If we place these mountains on the earth, it would reduce it to nothing. For someone like that, it does not fit to pretend to transcendence nor to the state of ultimate purity. Let the individual at least seek to rid himself of the burden of sins with which he has burdened himself!

Because there is a part of those people who have done wrong to themselves and then they have totally forgotten what they have done. They come to this *tariqa*, and then, when they contemplated the light of Allâh, they forgot their sins, they forgot their excesses and they thought to be among the people of the spiritual elevation.

No. Let's make things quite clear. I arrived in the *tariqa* at thirty or forty years old. So, I have to begin by considering, before reaching this *tariqa*: where have I dedicated my years of life? If I spent them in what offended the Lord, then I had to give thanks and to be grateful to this Way which was the cause of my moving away from those sins I used to commit.

However, we never see that. I have never seen a disciple who came to me and told me how much he had caused harm to himself in the past, how he had wasted his years, transgressed sacred things. But today *alhamduliLah*, since he had taken the *bay'a*, at least he was no longer making mistakes towards others or towards himself and he was invoking Allâh that this would be the door of his salvation, which would repair his past.

No. On the contrary. People believe that they are pure and purified. They imagine that they are chosen from among all human beings. They imagine, for example, that they are in the footsteps of Salman al-Farisiy, as the Prophet said: "*Salman al-Farisiy is part of people of my home (min ahli bayti).*"[41]

No my son! Wait... let's reconsider things as they have to be!

When you see that Salman al-Farisiy has a certain past, that he is coming from associators environment. Do not forget a thing, all along his life, since his puberty, he has never done anything else except looking for the *haqiqa*. In monasteries, in churches, with all those from whom he could smell this perfume of the esoteric knowledge. He spent his life going from hermitage to monastery and from monastery to hermitage, in order to reach the knowledge of the Creator. It is for this reason that when he reaches to the presence of Al-Mustafa, this one attested to him that

....

41 *Sifât as-safawa*, d'Ibn al-Jawzî.

he was part of the people of his house. Because since he had 10 years, he had never done nothing except seek this *haqiqa*. He was looking for this *qabda* of light.

You, you, you and you… no. Included myself who is talking to you. Let's be honest. You have not sought this in the past. On the contrary, you committed excesses against yourselves and you continue to do so. You were in the recklessness (*ghafla*) and you are still in it. This is the truth.

So now, the minimum, it is to bow down and to resign oneself to Allâh. Gratify Him and thank Him infinitely for ridding us of all those bad things that we used to do. One of these sins past that the *murid* was used to commit before, if he came down to the mountain of *Uhud*, he would pulverize it.

Stop thinking of yourself as one of the best, stop thinking of yourself as something incredible. When you hear "Ask yourself account before you are asked it", do it accurately and thoroughly. Do your accounting seriously. Read every line, all mistakes you have made.

Do not forget! Count everything since you were 10 years old. Count even the obligations. Did you do your prayers? Did you do all your prayers as you have to since 10 years old until today? The truth is you will realize only now that you make an effort to pretend since we are here to see you.

Count your fast, consider only the *maqam*[42] of *al-Islam*. Where are we in the *maqam* of *al-Imân* or *al-Ihsân*, did you really fast as you have to? Have you paid your *zakat*?

You know, I am a man of the 21st century, I know you well, I know where you come from, where you grow up. I

....

42 Meaning the station of al-Islam.

am not coming from the first century of the *hegira*. I am someone from among here, I have lived like you so even if you come to me doing all your drama, I cannot believe you. I know the state of the *murid* when he comes.

But, do not consider these past years, since you were 10 years old, let's consider only the time since you took the *bay'a*. Have you really been able to get rid of sins (*tajrîd*) completely since you took the *bay'a*? No...

For example, the one who has rid himself of the sin of fornication. If, effectively, he is no longer dating women, his eyes are still doing fornication. His ears fornicate, his tongue fornicates. His fingers, when he is chatting on the net, he is in the fornication of course!

So, let's start to set the record straight. Just on these basics. So, what should be said if I talk about hidden things as vanity (*al-kibr*), jealousy (*al-hasad*). Here just on the appearances, just what is manifesting if the *murid* was doing his count, he would realize that it brought him down to the depths of hell!

Dare to tell me the opposite... one by one, from the right to the left, as much as you are. No one can raise his hand and guarantee me that since he took the *bay'a*, he did not commit any apparent sin. Since the taking of the *bay'a*, based on the principle that *al-Islam* absolves mistakes of the past (in the case of a conversion). But for the repentant (*al-ta'ib*), we cannot say for him that *al-Islam* clears his past since he was already muslim! The *tawba*[43] has conditions: having regrets, stopping to commit the sin and repairing the harm caused to other. Have you given back what you

....

43 Meaning the repentance.

unfairly took to others!? Have you asked for forgiveness from those you have hurt? No, you are still full of pride.

Among you, they are people who have hurt their families, their neighbours, their friends... bring me one *murid* who, since he took the *bay'a*, has gone to ask forgiveness to someone after having hurt him. No, never, never! It is like he never did anything. He thinks that the *tawba* consists of saying *astaghfirullâh*. But this is only one door of the *tawba*! A door... because the *tawba* includes the three conditions mentioned above!

And you have to know that it is for this reason that you are not crying! Your eyes are dry! You can see disciples who never had one tear on their eyes! Why? Because his heart is dry! His heart is hard like a stone. How tears could flow from his eyes whereas he only sees on him purity, elevation and distinction!?

His eyes never cry, his heart never shudder whereas his tongue repeat the different phrases of *dhikr*. In the heart of *dhikr*, he thinks only to correct mistakes of others whereas he is the biggest of mistakes.

Going back to what we were talking about, what can we say about this *murid* that he is seeking the knowledge of Allâh? No, do not talk about *ma'rifa*. This person is still looking for the door of the *tawba* because the *tawba*, he still does not know how it works. He is looking for *tawba*, he is looking to get out of the darkness into the light.

Do you know the search of *ma'rifa*!? It is the search of the total purification of the heart. And how the Lord will clean this heart? Impossible for the Truth to clean a heart which does not shudder! A heart which does not shudder (*yakh-cha'*), it is a darkness heart, a black heart, a heart full of jealousy and hate. It is impossible to clean it with *lâ ilâha illa Allâh* or *astaghfirullâh*. Not because these words are not powerful enough but more because of the distance of the heart from the knowledge of what means *lâ ilâha illa Allâh*!

That's why, as al-Imam al-Ghazaly said: he is talking to you with the tongue of the *ma'rifa*. It means that he has this information (*khabar*) in himself and that he expresses but he does not taste it. Because the taste or the flavour (*dhawq*) of this discipline, it is in the depth of the heart (*al-fu'ad*) "the depth (*fou'âd*) did not deny what it saw"... not in the eyes!

You, you came to the *maqâm* of *al-Ihsân*, but you stayed at "I have seen the light of Allâh!"

Well, you have seen the light of Allâh. We did not say the opposite. The problem is that you have seen it with your eyes (*basar*)! But did you see it with your inner vision (*basîra*)? Have you seen it in the depth of your heart (*fu'ad*)? How to see it in your *fu'ad*?

It is very simple. If you had seen in your *fu'ad*, your heart would have shuddered (*khacha'a*) and your sins would have definitely disappeared. And your heart would have switched from one divine name to another.

Bring me back a disciple – since I came back from my trip a month and a half ago – bring me back a disciple, for example from those who left in *siyâha*, a disciple who would have come to see me and would have said "oh sidi Shaykh, this is what I understood from such and such verse or from such and such *hadith* or such and such day, when you made such and such *mudhâkara* for us, I understood that..."

Nothing at all! Neither in those who are present here, nor in those who are absent. There is nothing! No new understanding, no *tafsîr* of the Word of Allâh or the Sunna of the Prophet ﷺ. Why, while you see the light of Allâh!? Only because you do not interact with the light of Allâh. You are just watching the light.

When the *murid* wants to say something, he is only coming to impose his opinion. He does not come to return the branching to the origin, in order to bring out the branching from the origin.

No matter the domain you want to deal with, it can be technology, mathematics, physics, Quran, *sunna*, *fiqh* ... you have to come back to the original *qabda* of light.

Allâh is the light of the heavens and the earth.[44] The Lord did not let you any others doors. Whatever the thing, whatever the atom you will consider and you will want to study, send it back to the light of Allâh. Once you will do it, then make it return from the light of Allâh to you. Think about it, meditate with a quivering hear (*khachi'*), desiring only the face of the Lord, a heart looking for the knowledge of the Creator.

The one who wants Allâh, will never turn away from Allâh's words. The one who wants the prophet's presence ﷺ, will never turn away from the sunna of the Prophet ﷺ. The one who wants the *wilaya*, will never turn away from Allâh's people. It is simple, though.

But the disciple, he turns away from his Shaykh. His Shaykh himself, from whom he took the *bay'a*, he turns away from him! How can we say of him that he is presenting himself to Allâh and the prophet? No, it is impossible. Your Shaykh, the one who opened your heart, you turn

....

44   Surah an-Nur, verse 35.

away from him! You do not ask, you do not even ask your-self about the relationship you have with your Shaykh...

We are telling you that through the light you are return-ing the branching to the origin, and then from the origin you can get a branching. Just send your own branching (your being) back to your Shaykh... We are not going to look any further than that. Your Shaykh, you consider him as your origin. You consider him as your mirror. You con-sider him as the *haqiqa* of your body and your apparent form. Send me back even just your image, your apparent form! Give me even just a part of your apparent form! It means, concretely, erase your words and make what you say the words of your Shaykh. Erase your sight and make it the sight of your Shaykh. Erase your hearing and make it the hearing of your Shaykh. Erase your opinion... erase the catastrophe that are your thoughts and adopt the thoughts of your Shaykh. Erase your desires and adopt the desires of your Shaykh. But of course, you are incapable of that.

So, who are you? So can we say that you are fighting your Shaykh? Instead of being extinguished in him, you who come to make great speeches about what is not the *fana'*, you see the Shaykh, you are screaming "oh the *waliy* of Allâh!" then you go and kiss his hand and you imagine that it is that the *fana* or when you approach the presence of the prophet ﷺ and you say *as-salâmu 'alayka ya rasûlallâh*![45] coming with your arms and your legs imagining that it is done, you are in the presence of the prophet ﷺ.

No. Nothing to do with it. It is beyond all that. If you are claiming to want to interact with the prophet ﷺ then

....

45 Peace be upon you ô prophet.

manifest you own interior as being ahmadian, luminous, illuminate of a pre-eternal *qabla*... and let's appear his off-shoot meaning what is covering her and hiding her as being muhamadian meaning "a Quran which is walking".

This is in regard to the muhammadan *hadra*. Now in regard to the *hadra* of the Creator, you will have to manifest on one hand your own interior as being secret (*sirr*), the secret of the Creator's treasury. On the other hand, make appear what is manifested of yourself as His names, His attributes, His acts and His laws... until you see no existence of anything other than Him.

Find the flavour in your heart

Human being has the capacity to tame wild animals. You can, for example, tame a lion and make him obedient as a cat. However, look Nemrud as the king of his time, it is like if he tamed the world and what is on it except the mosquito who ended to drive him crazy. He had the power on everything but was not able to do anything against a simple mosquito!

Here, you understand that you can do what you want concerning what Allâh gave you. However, you have to know that you will never be able to exercise any power on a thing that He did not gave you beforehand. And you, Allâh decided to assign you to the Way (the *tariqa*). Henceforth He decided for you to count you among people of the Way. Stay (*aqim*) where Allâh place you in this Way, do not look for something else!

Allâh placed you in *al-tawba*? Stay in *al-tawba*.

Allâh placed you in *al-khidma*? Stay in *al-khidma*.

At least, Allâh assigned you something in this Way. Do not say "No, I do not like my situation…" because when you say that, you enter a whole new register. By saying that, it is like if you are saying "This *tariqa* is not for me". The problem, it is that you will never find something else. If you go out, if you leave the *tariqa*, where will you go? You will go in the ways which deviate it (*al-subul*).

So, the least we can do... as soon as I know where is the city of the science, if I cannot enter in it, at least, I will show *adab* concerning his door. Simply because I had the chance to find this door contrarily to others who are looking for it during their entire life without being able to attain it.

So, when you meditate on the creation of the heavens and the earth, as the Quran enjoin us to do, do not do it with the aim of seeing these heavens and this earth in your *qabda*, as sidi AbdelQader al-Jilaniy said. If Allâh assigned him to that, He assigned him to that, period. If he did not assign you to that, at least, stay in the constant practice of the *dhikr* since you have been designated to this *dhikr*. Never forget who you are. Never forget who you were. Never forget where do you come from. Invoke Allâh and maintain the good opinion of Him. This is how things have to be done.

Do not say "no, I did not understand anything about the pathway..." Since when you want to learn and understand the *tariqa* firstly? No, you do not want! You, you want to receive everything on a platter! You sit in front of the Shaykh during the course but do you even know why the Shaykh is giving you these courses!? It is not to give you information! These courses are not the teachings. No, he is giving you these courses to stir your hearts, to push you to think, to reflect, to meditate a little bit! So that you move forward properly on the path!

The Shaykh will not give you more than what you can receive. And what he is giving you is just enough to stimulate your heart and to stimulate it to move forward.

So, when the Shaykh talks, why am I not saying to myself that these words are coming from the origin and as a ramification, you are directly concerned? The best among you, if he thinks like that, if he thinks that Shaykh's words are directly directed to him, he takes his possessions and he leaves. He does not stay in these courses. He says that it burns him, he says "The Shaykh is talking about me..." and he flees. But no! Repairs what you broke rather! Do not break more what you broke until it becomes crumbs and will not serve anymore to anything!

No, when I realize that, when I consider that the Shaykh is talking to me directly, I have to follow this with the good reaction. If the Shaykh sends me a severe reprimand in his courses, the next time, I do not have to be the target on this same severe reprimand! I do not have to fall again on the same mistake twice! Because the disciples – all presents here, one by one – I can say to each of you how many times you repeat the same mistake. Always the same...

That means that the disciple does not even learn his own mistakes! His mistakes, he is repeating them, relentless, always the same. Then he is coming to ask solutions to the Shaykh. "Give me advices sidi Shaykh..." We already said everything to you! Once, twice, three times... every day I advise you! And you, you are on a loop... always... with the same mistake... always.

At least, if you let me the occasion to talk to you about another mistake that you are doing, to let you receive another advice... but no. Always the same thing from the morning to the night.

The smart, is one who understands with a simple look. But what do I mean "a simple look"? It means the shrill vision (*firasa*) of the faith. Simply because he is a believer and sincere in his pathway. And it is not a comprehension to understand, like we stock books in a library. No, it is a comprehension directly implemented, to correct us before it is too late.

The one who understand what we are saying to him but who does not correct himself, it is like if he did not understand anything.

This is how the *murid* has to move forward.

The *murid* has to look for his own reality (*haqiqa*). For example, he committed a mistake, he came in the *tariqa* and he did not know anything about the spiritual pathway. He committed this mistake... May he renew his *bay'a* right away.

Each time I do the *wird*, I have to renew my *bay'a*. I am doing it by magnifying (*ta'dhim*) the *wird* and his fruit (the light). Not like those who say "I am going to renew my intention; I am going to renew my *bay'a*..." whereas they even do not do the *wird* correctly or they do not give them the importance (*ta'dhim*) they deserve! I do not give importance to the *wird*, I am doing it anyhow and I pretend wanting to renew my *bay'a*? What *bay'a*? What are you talking about? Have you ever come to take *bay'a* to talk about renewal!?

The one who comes to renew his *bay'a*, he knows what he has done wrong! He knows what it means "to renew the *bay'a*", he knows that it is mandatory to correct his mistake.

But the disciple, what does he want? He wants to enter in the *tariqa* and to vanish directly as the *buraq*. Of course not, things are not so!

Look at me if we were not at the end of time, as the Prophet ﷺ says, where the one who will hold one-tenth of his religion will be equivalent to the one of the first generations who will hold in its entirely… this *tariqa* would never have existed!

Because the *tariqa*, as it has always been, the *murid* comes over to sit with the Shaykh during fifteen or twenty years to simply learn to endure the blows without saying "ouch". Nothing else! Just to learn receiving thumps without to sigh! It was not even about the light of Allâh… why?

The Shaykh did not give a light superior to the one of today. It was exactly the same. But why he did not give it to disciples in past centuries. Simply because the *murid* was not worthy yet. And why that? Because even if he had seen the light, he would not give it the importance (*ta'dhim*) that is due to it!

So, the Shaykh mishandled the disciple for years, even for decades… until he is feeling truly that the heart of the wayfarer become sweet, melted, lived by the ardent desire of the divine… after spending nights and nights to stay up and to implore the Lord then and only then, the Shaykh invoked Allâh in favour of his disciple and then this one could contemplate the divine light!

Then, the disciple remained like that during years with the light of Allâh until it establishes fully in his heart and only then, the Shaykh revealed to the disciple the secret of Allâh. It was possible only after truly testing the heart of the disciple and after being sure that there is any other dimension that the dimension which is required.

We, no, we know that you will not be able—particularly you the emigrant. You will not be able to stay in *tajrid* with the Shaykh. Anyway, the Shaykh has nothing to do with your *tajrid* because even those who are in *tajrid* here, they are not in *tajrid*. Even if you came here in *tajrid*, you will reproduce exactly the same thing than those who preceded you.

So, what do we tell you? We tell you at least to tie strongly to the light of Allâh and then we foster the good opinion concerning the *murid*, we tell us that maybe this one will not be as the others. Maybe this one will magnify the light and the secret of Allâh. We get rid of the responsibility and we tell you since the really beginning of your pathway: "Here you are, you and your Lord!" Only the maintenance of a good relationship (*ihsân*) between us and Him remains then, nothing else.

Why? Because we see the disciple already advanced in adulthood... the truth is that he does not have long to live. Am I still going to count with a disciple who is fifty or seventy years old? What do you want me to count with a sixty-year-old?

The sixty-year-old, in the divine law, he has only three years left to spend on earth. At the age of sixty-three, he must die. The one who lives beyond sixty-three years, it is only *nawâfil* for him. You should not plan to live beyond that. Do not project yourself for a century, you are not part of the community of *sayiduna* Nûh (*'alayhi salâm*)! You are part of the community of al-Mustafa ﷺ.

How old are you? Forty? So, you have twenty-three years to live. Make sure then you hold yourself accountable in the twenty-three years you have left. But no, the disciple is in total and absolute carelessness.

He is reckless (*ghafil*) concerning his life, concerning his sins, concerning all excess he committed against his own person...

Then indeed, we live with the disciple considering the *jamâl* that means that we say to ourself that the *tawba* and the good act (*hasana*) erase the bad works. Yes, but be careful, we are talking about *hasana*. The *hasana* or the virtuous work (*al-'amal as-sâlih*), Allâh elevates it, as He tells us in the Quran but it is the virtuous work free of ambiguity, free of zigzagging, free of any consideration of other than Him... the virtuous work that is exclusively accomplished for the Face of Allâh not the mixed work! Those works which are mixed with more evil than good! No, we cannot say that Allâh elevates these works.

If the prayer itself is not elevated... for some, their prayer rises an inch above their heads and for others, it does not rise at all. Others still, *masha Allâh*, so-and-so prays to *sidrat al-muntaha* in every one of their prayers... So, we cannot compare one with the other but everyone knows the value of his prayer. And this is not about mastering the gymnastics of the prayer. No, rather it is about to know whether or not I pray in the *qabda* of light. And if I pray in the *qabda* of light, do I really talk to it and address it through the Quran and the invocations?

When I prostrate in the *qabda* of light, do I really tell it: *Subhâna rabbi al-a'la*[46]? Or am I simply mastering the apparent performance and gestures of the *sujûd*, speaking, without even knowing to whom I am speaking? I have neither seen nor known the One to whom I am speaking...

....

46   Glorified be my Lord, the Most Hight.

I am merely repeating memorized formulas.

Where is the flavour (*dhawq*)?

The *dhawq* is in my heart, not on the prayer mat! It is in the heart, not in the gestures.

The gestures, the Lord has even exempted you from them! If you are sick, you can pray sitting down, or even lying down, you can pray with your eyes only. The appearances of the prayer can be subject to dispensations unlike the inner reality of the prayer, which has no dispensation. You may not be able to accomplish something apparent but what is within you, you have no excuse, and that is the most important thing.

Ô sufi, do you see your Lord?

Allâh ﷻ says: **We will show them Our signs in the horizons and within themselves until it becomes clear to them that it is the truth.**[47]

In the universe and within themselves. All wayfarers towards Allâh by His Light include concretely this intrinsic link between the human soul and the universe: When the theophanic Light is reaching you, you say "I see in my heart a Star" and likewise in the universe there are stars.

You say: "I see a Sun", "I see galaxies", "I see creatures" and as well as in the end, you are finding in yourself all the universe. Therefore, the first part of the verse is included and realized for all of you (karkary disciples).

What about the second part? **...until it becomes clear to them that it is the truth.** To understand that, you have to revert to the story of *sayiduna* Ibrahim (*'alayhi salâm*): **We also showed Abraham the wonders of the heavens and the earth, so he would be sure in faith. When the night grew dark upon him, he saw a star and said, "This is my Lord!"**[48]

When *sayiduna* Ibrahim (*'alayhi salâm*) saw the Star, he saw it with the degree of "those who believe with belief" and in opposite to you, he did not say: "This is a star" but

....

47   Surah Fussilat, verse 53.
48   Surah al-Anam, verses 75 and 76.

well and truly: **This is my Lord!** because he truly realized the evidence of what it is, al-Haqq! You say that you see the Star because you did not realize that yet. You do not have then the complete verse, only the first part.

It is by realizing fully that the contemplating is no one except the contemplated himself that it will **become clear [to you] that this is al-Haqq**. Ibrahim (*'alayhi salâm*), the prophet and messenger between the elite of Allâh's messengers (*olo l-'azm*), the one who is in the seventh sky, leant to *al-bayt al-ma'mour* (the filled home), the filled home of treasures of the Allâh's knowledge ﷺ.

But what does the ignorant say?

Full of arrogance, he affirms that *sayiduna* Ibrahim did a mistake, what is more a mistake that directly affects the *Tawhid*... well, correct him! Ô you who is in this earth, correct the one who is in the seventh sky, leant to *al-bayt al-ma'mour*!

Look for the reason of your creation?

"Ô mankind, reuniting in him all the characteristics of perfection and imperfection... Ô mankind, veiled from yourself by yourself... Exalted be the transcendence of The One who created you by making Himself appear, from yourself in yourself and for yourself, shaping through you the mirror of absolute perfection!"

O mankind, what has deceived you concerning your Lord, the Generous? Who created you, fashioned you, and perfected your design, moulding you in whatever form He willed.[49]

It is the verse seven of the surah al-Infitâr. In other words, ô mankind, when will you know the constitution of your being, your specificities and the reason of your creation? When you will accomplish the seventh readings! The verse seven... the Lord could have made this verse the third or the fourth of the surah. But no, it is the seventh so that you understand that it is a question here for you to return and to accomplish these seven readings. Then, you will be able to know your *haqiqa* pursuant to the verse: "*There certainly has come to you a messenger from among yourselves.*"[50]

....

49 Surah al-Infitâr, verse 7.
50 Surah at-Tawab, verse 128.

You who pretend to the *ma'rifa* and to the divine proximity, you who pretend to the *nafsiya* of al-Rahman, to the *nafsiya* of al-Mustafa ﷺ... what does the Lord say about this *nafs*?

O reassured soul, return to your Lord, well-pleased and pleasing [to Him], so join My servants.[51]

So join My servants. If she is entering, she is entering as a result of her full state of servitude (*'ubudiya*), after having risen through three secrets. She knew the reality of this pre-eternal proximity and she came back under the form of a complete, finalized *nafs* and so could enter among the servants. She did not enter in what is linked to the carelessness (*ghafla*), neither the distance (*bu'd*). Rather, she entered in the one who loved her Lord as she has to.

From there, he made sprout in him the science and the esoteric knowledge (*ma'rifa*), in accordance with the continuity of the verse: **So join My servants, and enter My Paradise.** that means the paradise of the esoteric knowledges. So, the person becomes one of those to whom Allâh has forgiven what has preceded and what is yet to come.

That being said, in accordance with what the state of servitude requires, you must always fear Allâh because even if Adam was in heaven... and as we know, in the heaven, you are free to do whatever you want ... everything except the tree! Be careful. Do not approach it and do not go to serve you in it! And I fear that this tree is the blessed Tree itself. This Tree which is such that if you approach it and intend to serve it without permission (*idhn*), it will make you fall to the lowest degrees, as it raised you to the highest.

....

51   Surah al-Fajr, verse 27-29.

At the bottom, you will fall again to the four directions where you will seek your true *nafs*: Hawwa'[52]. You will say to yourself: "Maybe I will find it in Iraq or in India or in the far north...". But it is finally on the Mount 'Arafa that you will meet up through the *fana* in the *alif al-muqaddar*, in a long path of return to the Lord, a path of efforts in the seventh readings of the divine Name... seventh readings which will show you terminate in the *alif al-muqaddar*, with your own *nafs*. And then, what will you do? You will implore the divine forgiveness and you will weep.

----

52   Hawwa is Eve in Arabic.

Your heart makes you either
a beloved of Allâh or a shaytân

Instead of sowing the discord by taking care of things which are exterior to yourself, work to the purification of your heart: empty it of the consideration of everything except Him and make it return to his Lord. In this way, you will make good your hand, your intellect, your thought... our Lord saying in that sense in the *hadith* of the *waliy*:

"*The servant does not draw near to Me with anything more loved to Me than the religious duties I have obligated upon him. And My servant continues to draw near to me with nafil (supererogatory) deeds until I love him. When I love him, I am his hearing with which he hears, and his sight with which he sees, and his hand with which he strikes and his foot with which he walks...*"[53]

When the servant loves another servant, what does he like him with? With the hand? No... with the foot? No... with the tongue? No... He loves with the heart, of course! So, when the heart is good, the love flows in him.

Now, think about your state: to whom is devoted the love in your heart? You love your wife, your mother, your son, your neighbour, the *dunia*, the business... but you do not have the love of Allâh. We have to say things clearly.

....

53   Hadith *qudsi* related by al-Bukhari.

This is why you cannot have the control on your hand. Your hand does whatever it wants. Your foot does whatever it wants. Your eye does whatever it wants…

If you reached to empty your heart and if you attained truly the *hadith* of the *waliy* then you will not act anymore only for and with the love of Allâh. And it is by this love that the whole limbs of your body would become good. So, if you remark that you do not have the control of your own hand …

For example, someone who cannot avoid to steal, as soon as he sees something he likes, he takes it. Or someone who cannot control his look: as soon as a woman walks besides him, he has to look at her. As soon as a debauched show herself, he cannot avoid to observe her and to linger on her unbridled.

Ô you, you have to know that your heart is sick! Here, you know that your heart is bad then do not come and pretend to the love of Allâh!

The tongue… as soon as you sit to talk, you are only using a foul and vulgar language… "and so-and-so this, and so-and-so that…" you did not spare no one in the *ummah*, you roasted all the country. You have to know that your heart is fundamentally bad!

Now, let's consider the opposite case… The one who has a pure heart, the clearest of his time, he is silent. He is not pretending to be a kind of person in front of some people to seem well while with others, he is the opposite… No. When he talks, he talks about his Lord and when he is silent, he meditates about what his Lord do with His creation. That means that he is always busy. Do you get it?

Even if we talk with him about *dunia's* things, it is not that he is not listening to you, no... rather, he thinks about the organisation of all of that. You, you are talking to him about the *dunia*, you are talking about business, marriage etc. He thinks about that and answer to you by giving you an interpretation, delivering you a link (*wasl*) about the solution which escape you. And you, you stay amazed because indeed, it is alongside him that you can find the solution to your problem. This is because he is the one who is the closest to the *haqiqa*, the closest to the *wasl*. As for you, your thought is cartesian, your though is limiting to "my hand", "my foot" that is why you are unable to find solutions to your life's issues.

You are drawing in yourself and the worst, really the worst disaster, it is that despite all that, you are still pretending to be an example of righteousness: you are the imam, you are the leader, you are the guide, you are the strong, you are the capable... this is the real disaster, the one who has no cure.

If only... if only you felt this weakness, this failure, this inability which afflict you... if only you could see and consider people who are around you as being better than you... then, you will feel ashamed about yourself and you will know, you will realize how much far you are!

You, no, you are not there, not at all: "Me, I pray, I fast..." whereas from the morning to the night, you are doing back and forth in the markets... talking about this one, criticizing this other... You ate the flesh of everybody, you did not spare any one! You ate more darkness than can never gulp your stomach as food. Because, as you know, the one who talk on the backs of others, it is like if he ate their flesh once dead... so my dearest one, consider your state and how much quantity of meat you gulp each day... you dare after that pretend being among Lord's beloved?

Start by mending some order in your life. Your hand, it is the same thing... when will these hands become His hand with which He strikes? And this foot, His foot with which He walks? When will your hearing become the hearing of the Truth? When will your sight become the sight of the True? This is why you cannot see the Light of Allâh! That is why when you saw someone reaching to that and begins to perceive these inspirations (*hâtif*) of the Lord, you, you deny it. Why? Because you are dived in the carelessness (*ghafla*) and in the veil of your corporality.

So, to resume, what is *ghafla*? It is your body.

What is the solution? It is its fundamental basis (*manba'*): your heart. If you purify the fundamental basis of your body, the water which circulate on him will be a clean and pure water.

Does not the Messenger of Allâh say: "*Certainly, the Shaytân is flowing in the human being through his veins.*"[54] In other words: your hand become Shaytân, your foot become Shaytân, your eye become Shaytân... because the veins so the blood, there are in all the body! But if you impose limits to your heart, if you reach to embrace by the *dhikr*, by the meditation, by the good behaviour... what will happen?

Your hand will start to worry the Lord. Your hearing will fear Allâh so that even if you came to sit with someone, you

....

54 *Sahih* al-Bukhari and *Sahih* Muslim.

will advise him like you have. If he commits the slander or if he slurs, you provide him the good advice. Of course, the advice has to come from a soft and subtle tongue obviously considering you tongue would be the tongue of the True.

Thus, the person will only see the Light because he will become himself entirely Light: his heart will be Light, his hearing will be Light, his sight will be Light and so on.

In that sense, someone asked to the messenger of Allâh ﷺ if he seen his Lord and he replied: "*He is a Light that I saw at this moment.*"[55] in other words: "I am completely submerged in the Light of the Lord.".

If he had said for example: "When I do the *dhikr*, I see the Light of Allâh", or "When I pray, I see the Light of Allâh" then this vision would have been specific to a time and a place in default of some others.

Through his word ﷺ: "*He is a Light that I see right now*", we understand that he is constantly submerged in the contemplation of the divine Light. That is the indication of the state of complete Presence and this is not exclusively reserved to the Messenger of Allâh ﷺ exclusive of others... no. On the contrary, that is true for his whole community. Because what was ordered him to accomplish devolve to the whole community ﷺ.

....

55 *Ibid.*

Wake up, you are reckless

When the *adhan* of the morning's prayer sounds... it is absolutely inconceivable that the suitor to the spirituality is, at this moment, in the toilet emptying his stomach... When the *adhan* of the morning sounds, you should have prayed two *rak'at*, sitting in the direction of the *qibla* waiting for the call. This is for those who fail to perform their duty of *qiyam al-layl*. As for those who do it, they have already been up for an hour. But make sure that when the *adhan* is heard, you are on the prayer mat. And those who do not perform *qiyâm al-layl*, truly, it is a shame to wake up after the *adhan* or for the *adhan* to be done while you are in the toilet!

How would we answer to *mu'adhin* as the sunna wants it whereas we are in the toilet, emptying our stomach or doing our ablutions? In a hadith, it says that when the *adhan* of the morning's prayers sounds, an angel is sent to the one who is sleeping and says to him: "Wake up, you reckless!" He does not say: "Wake up, ô believer" neither "Wake up, ô muslim". This is the word of *sayiduna* al-Mustafa ﷺ, so no conjecture to add on this topic.

So that means that if you are sleeping during the hour of the *adhan*, you are automatically stamped and sealed "reckless (*ghafil*)" whereas you initially, you come to the *zawiya*, looking for awakening.

It is you who are looking for righteousness, it is you who are looking for the knowledge of your Lord so why to lie to one-self? You are pretending to looking for that but at the time of *adhan*, you are sleeping. You are *ghafil* and since the moment the angel stamped you as *ghafil*, it is not the Shaykh who will remove it you!

You have to be aware concerning that.

If you are *ghafil*, it is stamped. Henceforth, do not come interfere among people of awakening because you have been stamped: "Wake up, ô reckless!" ... even if you would wake up to pray! Because the most important moment to not miss, it is exactly the moment of the *adhan*. It is at this moment that the degrees are spread: it is at this moment that muslims differ from people of *imân* and people of *ihsân*. It is at the moment of the *adhan* and particularly the *adhan* of *sobh*.

And why we insist constantly on the prayer of *sobh*? Because it is about the *salât al-wusta*: **Observe the five obligatory prayers—especially the middle prayer.**[56] It is about the prayer of *sobh*. So, of course, there are scholars who defended other opinions... in particular that it is about the prayer of *'asr* but what would prevent you to pray *'asr* to be enjoined to be keen to it? The easiest prayer it is precisely *'asr*! At the moment you pray *dhohr*, you pray *'asr*, it is in the continuity. But the prayer of *sobh* no, it is difficult... and this is why Allâh insists about it. Because at this hour, you are inclined to sleep... whereas for all others prayers, you are already awake. It is only the prayer of *sobh* which involved a rest period.

....

56   Surah al-Baqarah, verse 238.

Furthermore, *sayiduna* al-Mustafa ﷺ did not do the *mi'raj* at the time of *'asr*, neither at the time of no others prayers of the day. The *mi'raj* takes place in the last third of the night. That means at the hour of *sobh*. So, if you have also the pretention to looking for the *mi'raj*, consider your state, ô *murid*! Ô you who is looking for the accomplishment of the *mi'raj*, you who aspire to elevate your spirit, to see and to contemplate the superior worlds, the Messengers, the Prophets... whereas you do not even have the prayer of *sobh*!?

When will you do the *mi'raj*? At one o'clock of the afternoon maybe!? It is impossible, forget that right now.

In your inner-self, you are submerged by doubts: why the Shaykh wears a *subha* around his neck? But you, why you do not pray *sobh* hourly? We, when we point at some aspects of your behaviour, we are doing it by the *shari'a* unlike you... it is there that you can see that the level of *shari'a* that you have on your head, it is zero!

So, listen carefully: You who are looking for the elevation and the purification of the soul, this work has to be done during the last third part of the night. It is mandatory!

For me, when I went out of the *khalwa*, the Shaykh did not constraint me to stay up the last third part of the night. He said to me that with my own spiritual degree, if I am saying three times "Allâh" when I wake up, it is enough. But me, I do not say to you to wake up and say three times "Allâh", I am telling you to wake up and to do the *qiyyam* during one hour! Because you did not reach yet this spiritual degree in which you just need to mention Him three times and that it is for you equal to one hour of the *qiyyam*. You can stay up the entire night... since *al-'isha* until *sobh* and without guarantee, see yourself what's going on. I am not saying that I am better than you, no. In this state where I was, when the Shaykh was alive, the spiritual aspiration (*himma*) was very very high. I was waking up at midnight then I was beginning and I did not sleep until *dhohr* where I was doing a nap of one hour. You, if you only turn off your laptop at midnight, it will already be a good thing.

When I was in the phase of the spiritual education (*tarbiya*), I was putting my alarm at midnight, I was doing my ablutions, two *raka'at* and I was beginning... I was doing my program of nights prayers that no one here is doing yet because nights prayers have a program, there are specifics things according the day of the week etc. To accomplish them, you need one hour to begin. If you do these prayers, you would not have the time to do the *dhikr*. So, for now, we let a complete and reserved hour exclusively for the mention of the name of "Allâh". We set the phone on one hour then we put it under the pillow and when he is vibrating one hour after, we know that we did one hour of *dhikr*, without opening eyes neither doing anything else except merge and disappear into the light. This is what we are looking for during this hour. Before that, it is an hour of prayers, one hour dedicated to the adoration.

I am saying that to those who are looking for the *khalwa*: "I want the *khalwa*, I want that, I want this..." So, show us!? How many times I come down the night and I find you sleeping? Just yesterday, when did you pray *sobh*? You think I do not know? I am upstairs: we can hear everything. And then, they come to say that the Shaykh does not pray *sobh*! Because you, you pray it right!?

But you, no. At this moment, we cannot neither touch you, neither talk to you, neither nothing... you have to know that you did not pray *sobh*! And if you waste the time of *sobh*, the time of all others prayers are wasted too: the train has passed, it is too late.

Stop wasting your time

The name "Allâh" is written for Allâh's people, as you can see it above my head, with the *lâm* split in two... this *lâm al-qabd*, you constate that there is a darkness isthmus (*barzakh*). Or like if letters are all from light and that this darkness splitted this *lâm* in two parts.

First, you worked and you progressed thanks to the light. You learnt how to dive and to erase yourself in the ocean of lights. You realized that this ocean was the pre-eternal ocean, the ocean of deep senses, the ocean which is serving you as an interface (*barzakh*) between you and al-Rahman.

Now, you have to remind yourself, about your relation with the darkness. You have to come back to this darkness in order to understand them. Because you cannot understand what is the day if you do not know what is the night. You cannot know what is the immobility (*al-sukun*) without knowing what is the movement (*al-haraka*).

Also, you cannot know the reality of this light only and only if the Shaykh is showing you your darkness. Since the beginning, the Shaykh did not make you go through any fear or fright. On the contrary, he gave you the light and since, you only progress by the light: *salâm qawlan min rabbin rahîm.*[57]

....

57 **Salam (peace be on you)—a Word from the Lord (Allâh), Most Merciful.** Surah Yasin, verse 58.

Problems of darkness did not touch you or did not affect you in any way. If the Shaykh showed you what are your darkness then gave you an only atom of the light, you will certainly become aware of his importance. Because darkness, what are inside them?

We find in it Iblis and his associates. All the *shayâtîns*. All things that your thoughts can imagine as *soufli* atrocity. Darkness are multiples, they are systematically employed in plural. That means that as soon as you will see something scary, they will show you that more scary things are existing, more than what you can never imagine.

As for you, what pushed you to underestimate and depreciate the *tariqa*, it is that you were able to access to the light so easily. It did not cost you anything. You were not afraid by any monster or darkness creatures.... You come to everything all at once.

So, imagine a little bit... who are you?

If you despise this light, if it never had any effect on you, who could you possibly be? You have to know that this light is al-Mustafa ﷺ! As for you, you are darkness! That means that all things that scared you, know that you are scarier! You are afraid of from this darkness gush a shaytân or a monster but you ignore that you are, yourself, scarier than anything you could ever see!

This shaytân, unless him, he did not despise the light unlike you who did not stop doing it. This is your *haqiqa*.

It is for this reason that in the *lâm al-qabd*, we find this slot of darkness. And that is where your location is, in this *lâm al-qabd*. Do not think that your fluctuation (*sarayân*) in the *lâm* would be similar to your fluctuation in the light (as it was the case in the *hâ'*). No, your fluctuation in the *lâm al-qabd* will begin with a progression in the darkness. To let you know, to let you realize that you are only darkness.

Then, you will bow down with a total prostration for the True ﷻ. You will know the value of this light and you will hope that just an atom remains in you. It is at this moment that you will act toward the light as you have to, meaning as you have to act with the Prophet himself ﷺ!

So welcome to the *lâm al-qabd*: your spirit will have certainly been caught (*qubidat*) and you will live a true relation between you and the Prophet ﷺ. You will become yourself an image, an apparent form of this original light. You are not, actually, an apparent form of this original light and you will become it only when you will realize that your *haqiqa* is only pure darkness. When it will be done, your states will become so terrible that you will cry, day and night, without being able to breathe neither at home nor outside.

As for you, who are still eating as you please, drinking and forgetting yourself... know that you have not yet known your *nafs*. The grave is either a hole of hell or a garden of heaven. If you stick to that, the *haqiqa* will reveal itself to you little by little, through matter because the truth is that you have never had faith in anything but physical matter. You have never had faith in the deeper meaning or in the *haqiqa*.

So, the reality of your *nafs* will reveal to you in the obscurity of the grave and you will obviously find it scary. The truth is that nothing nor exterior person to yourself will have afraid you: you would simply scare yourself. It is only your *haqiqa* which is scary!

However, if you knew to greet this light by magnifying it, by sacralising it and by praising the Lord for her, then your grave will become a garden of heaven and nothing nor person exterior to yourself is the cause of this joy. You will enjoy about yourself, by yourself, because you reached to fix yourself, you and all the members which are in fact your only family.

It is why I tell you: do not lose your time! Instead of loosen up, instead of give up yourself to the reckless, wallow yourself in the *dunia*... one day will come where we will pray on you the death prayer and you will not escape it.

Without act, no knowledge

Each person aspiring to the openness of his intellect (*'aql*) will have to begin by shaping his body. That means make it conforms to the divine plan and to what he was created for. By the intermediary of the body, it is possible for us to constraint the intellect and to push it to the spiritual realization as well as the esoteric Knowledge (*ma'rifa*).

This is done through the exercise and efforts of worship, by persisting relentlessly in the accomplishment of those works that allow the purification of this intellect... and these works, it is indeed the body that performs them. It is made to do the *khalwa*, the *dhikr*, the *siyâha*, the *hadra* and so on and that until its intellect reach to grape the *ma'rifa* and what reveals the domain of the unknown (*ghayb*).

However, if the body is not constraint and acclimated to these exercises, if he denies it following by that the tendency of the *nafs* of his passions or following what his *qârin* and his *waswas* inject on him... this one has, obviously, no part in the knowledge of the different degrees of the intellect.

It is the same for the esoteric sciences: when the person is persisting, years after years by going to school every day, by being focus on the class, by doing his homework after the class and so on, it is thanks to all these exercises and to all these constraint, physical and intellectual that the comprehension of the student is expanding, that he can progress and learn years after years. Only the perfectly ignorant can deny that!

Because the ignorant, always, he is waiting... he does not move, he does not work, he does not do anything. He imagines that things will come from their own so he is waiting and he says "My Lord is the Forgiving and the most Merciful!" It is always by this door that he enters, like if it was about a protector veil for him, an excuse on which he took a break.

Regarding the one who is thinking, working and making efforts, he sacrifices himself body and soul, he constraints himself to the education and after only, he permits himself to believe on what the ignorant pretends: "My Lord is the Forgiving and the most Merciful!"

As long as *dunia* is in your hand, it is in your heart

Allâh ﷻ says: **Allâh has indeed purchased from the believers their lives and wealth in exchange for paradise.**[58]

So, consider your state and see where you are in terms of giving away your possessions (*nafaqa*) and in terms of selling your *nafs*.

Are you or are you not able to abandon the shadow of your being, to erase and disappear in the Light of the Lord? In the Light of the Lord, there is no money, nor *nafs*. The Light of the Lord is a breath of the Spirit, pure and immaculate. If you have in your pocket an only *dirham*, the *Diwan* will not accept you in his midst. Get rid of this *dirham* and then come and enter in the divine Presence.

If your *nafs* is always preoccupied by your wife, your daughter and you son: the access to the *Diwan* will not be allow for you. Get ride of your *nafs* and then come and enter in the divine Presence.

In the *Diwan* of the Lord, there is nothing except **Light upon Light, Allâh guides to His light whom He wills.**[59]

....

58   Surah at-Tawba, verse 111.
59   Surah an-Nur, verse 35.

And only people of the total and absolute purification by the divine Light can access it. Of course, nothing could blemish those people.

Spare us words like "the *dunia* is in my hand, not in my heart!"... the language of "specialists". Forget that immediately!! Do not even pronounce it in the presence of *ahl Allâh*! The *dunia* will not leave your heart as long as it will not have left your hand! As long as it is in your hand, the *dunia* is in your heart! It is only by wrenching it from your hand that you would discard your heart of it. And it is only at this moment that you will begin to realize its true value, you will begin to taste the Handful of Light that you have in your heart and that you could access to the *Diwan*.

Then and only then, go and take whatever you want from the *dunia* as well as *sayiduna* Sulaymân (*'alayhi salâm*) did it: when he dived within the Luminous Presence, he vanished and disappear completely in it, he said: **My Lord, forgive me and grant me a kingdom such as will not belong to anyone after me.**[60]

Then, indeed, the wind was subjected to him, the mountains were subjected to him... even the *shayâtin* were acting only under his orders! All this obviously by the Permission of Allâh ﷻ, but this happened only after *sayiduna* Sulaymân (*'alayhi salâm*) had reached the Handle of Exclusive Light and dived into it with a total and absolute dive.

Your part in the spiritual dimension will not only be dependent of, and in proportion to, your immersion and your erasure in the Light. So, consider your state: Did you really kill yourself, a total death? Did you really realize the

....

60   Surah Sad, verse 35.

death? Did you really die before you died? Did you really ask yourself before you were asked? Once it is done, welcome to you in the Presence of the Lord ﷻ.

It is not about being drown in the carelessness (*ghafla*), never do the *dhikr* then come to see me and say: "ah… sidi Shaykh, get me out of this state…" like it was the case with a disciple who came, recently and said to me that he could not evoke anymore the Name of Allâh. Is that so? You cannot evoke anymore the Name? No! In fact, it is not you who cannot evoke anymore the Name but it is the Name who does not want you! Because you are impure!

The verse says: **Allâh intends only to remove from you the impurity [of sin], O people of the [Prophet's] household, and to purify you with [extensive] purification.**[61]

Ahl al-bayt are people of the Presence, people of the Luminous Handful, they are not blemished, they are not reached by the impurity. They are immaculately pure: such are the *ahl al-bayt*. *Ahl al-Ka'ba*, the people of the House of *sayiduna* al-Mustafa ﷺ. *Ahl al-bayt al-Haqq* ﷻ, *Ahl al-bayt al ma'moûr*! They are the ones who enter in it, they are the ones who reach the state of intimacy, following the example of *sayiduna* Ibrahim (*'alayhi salâm*).

But who is *sayiduna* Ibrahim (*'alayhi salâm*)? He is the one who believed and put faith in his dream. See the difference! *Sayiduna* Ibrahim, the intimate of Allâh, he put faith in a thing that he saw in his dream. As for you, you did not even put faith on what you see in awake state! *Sayiduna* Ibrahim (*'alayhi salâm*) put faith in a dream that he saw when he was sleeping… you, your eyes are open, you do

....

61   Surah al-Ahzab, verse 33.

dhikr and then when you close them, you see the Light of Allâh but you do not even put any truth and faith in the *mushahâda*...

What else can we bring you? What are we going to do with you!?

You, become Ibn ʿArabi

The Messenger of Allâh ﷺ says: "*Die before to die.*"[62]

When you die, a complete and total death… not a death after which you continue to think of your little person, your money and so on… no, you are dead! The one who is dead, does he come back to think about these things? No, he only thinks about what is waiting for him!

When the dead man is washed, he does not think about what the cleaner is doing to his body but rather where his spiritual degree will lead him. He is afraid and he is terrorized for all its shortcomings and all things that he did not do correctly. When the dead man is washed, he does not come back to think about what he left… "Oh my son… Oh my wife…. Oh my home…".

No all these things, he does not see them anymore, he does not think about it anymore. He does not see anything else except the *fass* (the jewel of the ring) under which he will be found: the compilation (*khazîna*) of divines Names to which he will have reached.

This is what he will think about. And if you are able to feel that here, in this world: to you the *maʾrifa*!

If you are able, like the dead, to forget absolutely all these things and to focus exclusively on what come in front of you, it means this Original *Qibla* (the Point of Light), at

....

62 Reported by par al-ʾAjloûniy in *Kashf al-Khafa.*

this moment, even if you only pronounce just once "Allâh", or *astaghfirullâh*, or *lâ hawla wa la quwata illa billâh*[63] or if you did only one prayer on *sayiduna* al-Mustafa ﷺ, it will be enough!

It is He who confers blessing upon you, and His angels that He may bring you out from darkness into the light.[64]

Pray at least just one prayer like they prayed on you your Lord and His angels and you will remain enjoying the Lights for eternity.

However, if you are not able to do that, then you are just establishing an exchange or barter link: it is a win-win. Repeat a thousand times, ten thousand times, one hundred thousand times... so that in the end there is a chance that 1% of what you have said has been pronounced with the required strength.

If you are stingy and do not give alms, then you must do a lot of *dhikr*. Based it on the hadith: according to Abu Hureyra, the Prophet ﷺ said: "*The dhikr is better than alms*". If you rely on this, you have to accomplish a lot of *dhikr*! Until your tongue is softened by the evocation of Allâh, your heart is softened and your eyes cry. At this moment even if you do not take like the first one (the one who gives everything he has), you will still receive a very big share.

So see which door you will enter through. Do not go trying to get in through a door with small steps imagining that you will become an-Nabulsi or ibn 'Arabi! Go read the life of ibn 'Arabi!

....

63 *Astaghfirullâh:* I seek forgiveness from Allah. *Lâ hawla wa la quwata illa billâh:* there is no power and no strength except with Allah.
64 Surah al-Ahzab, verse 43.

Of course, you like *al-Foutouhât al-Makkiya, al-Rasâ’il al-Ilahiya*... but if you want to become as him then do like he did! Give up everything, go until Mecca and stay there a complete year. Or do as al-Hallâj: a piece of bread in your turban, a glass of water in hand and do the *tawaf* around the Ka’aba in fasted state during a complete year!

Of course, you cannot do that, you do not have the strength! At least, stay awake the night! That is the minimum, stay awake the last third of the night!

You, you did not do as al-Hallâj, nor as Ibn ‘Arabi, you did not even do the *qiyâm layl* nor anything at all! You sleep, you snore, and the *ma’rifa* must come down anyway! It is not possible! So, of course the *waswas* and the doubts get to you! Of course, the darkness overwhelms you! But if you reach to this degree... this degree where you walk, barefoot, naked, without owning anything, neither what is in front of you, neither what is behind you then the divine providence will manifest to you and, indeed, you will really enter in the degree of *tawakkul*, the absolute surrender in Allâh.

You will communicate with the entire universe. Trees and stones will talk to you. The sky and the water will talk to you. They will tell you their time, how it was and how it has become. You will discover their secrets, and the Wisdom of it all, without even needing to make *dhikr*. Just from time to time you will say *subhânAllâh, astaghfirullâh, lâ hawla wa la quwata illa billâh*, and you will outperform the one who will sit and stay day and night in front of the *qibla*, dedicating all his time to *dhikr*.

Talk to your heart

Regarding the deep senses of the full realization (*al-kamâl*), there are the *asmâ' al-husnâ*. And these names come back to al-Mustafa ﷺ, because Allâh ﷻ Himself qualified him by His names in the Quran. You cannot deny it in any way. Allâh called him *ra'ûf* (compassionate) and *rahîm* (merciful). Al-Ra'ûf and al-Rahîm are names of Allâh ﷻ but it is by them that He described al-Mustafa ﷺ.

He described him too as being *karîm* (generous) and *chahîd* (witness) and He even said: **Indeed, those who pledge allegiance to you, they are actually pledging allegiance to Allâh.**[65] The *bay'a* you took from al-Mustafa ﷺ is a *bay'a* taken from Allâh ﷻ.

Thus, extend the limits of your intellect if you have an intellect. In all this, there is no disclosure of any secret. I am not speaking in an intellectual dimension; I am only reporting what Allâh ﷻ has said!

If you do not believe in these clear verses, then tear them out of the Quran!

All this, it is what the Lord presented to us clearly. He says thus: **Indeed, those who pledge allegiance to you, they are actually pledging allegiance to Allâh.** surah al-Fath and it is the verse ten! That means that in him were

....

65 Surah al-Fath, verse 10.

united and fully realized the ten readings, so that the one who took the *bay'a* from him, truly took *bay'a* from Allâh ﷻ Himself.

He ﷻ named him with what He names Himself and in the *shahâda*, the testimonial of *ach-hadu allâ ilâha illa Allâh*[66] is only valid if it is accompanied by *wa ach-hadu anna Muhammadan rassûlullâh.*[67] This ultimate specificity has not been granted to any others creatures.

In others parts of the Quran, He does not even do the distinction between the two names: **Allâh—as well as His Messenger—has greater right that they should please Him (*yurdûh*).**[68] He did not say: "Allâh and His messenger HAVE greater right that they should please THEM (*yurdûhumâ*)." From this, we have to understand that whoever who satisfies Allâh, he satisfies the Messenger of Allâh ﷺ. Inversely, the one who satisfies the Messenger of Allâh, satisfies Allâh.

Also, Allâh says: **O believers! Respond to Allâh and His Messenger when He calls you to that which gives you life**[69] and He did not say: "O believers! Respond to Allâh and His Messenger when THEY call you (*da'awkum*)".

So here again, we understand that if the Messenger of Allâh ﷺ calls you, it is Allâh ﷻ who calls you and if Allâh ﷻ calls you, it is the Messenger of Allâh ﷺ who calls you.

....

66 I attest that there is no God except Allâh.
67 And I attest that Muhammad is the prophet of Allâh.
68 Surah at-Tawba, verse 62.
69 Surah al-Anfal, verse 24.

In this, the True ﷻ gives us an indication that what the names "Allâh" and "*al-rassûl*" refer to, have only one and same meaning (*ma'nâ*), and only one and same reality (*haqîqa*).

But even more than all this, here is a verse even harsher than the previous ones. A verse in which Allâh orders him to attribute to himself the servants: **Say, "O My servants who have transgressed against themselves, do not despair of the mercy of Allâh."**[70] and He did not say: "Say: "Ô servants of Allâh!""

These verses are clear and there are so many which have the same sense in the Quran, here, they are only examples. From that, what do you find surprizing in the secret of Allâh, in the *hâ al-hawiya* or in the *lâm al-qabd* or in the *lâm al-ma'rifa* or in the *fasl* and the *wasl* and in the lecture of *alif al-muqaddar* through the different spiritual presences (*hadarât*) of the prophets and messengers?

What is so amazing and incredible about this?

By Allâh Almighty, what is absolutely incredible is your ignorance! Because if you had opened the Quran, if you really have been among those who tasted the secret, you would find this secret clear as day in the Book of Allâh. You could not have denied it in any way.

What push you to deny it? It is your ignorance, your stupidity. I want you to look in the mirror and see written in big letters on your own reflection: "*Jâhil*" (ignorant). You read the Quran or rather you pretend to read the Quran then you come and you ask me: "Why the secret is like this... why I did not understand it like that...".

....

70 Surah az-Zumar, verse 53.

SubhânAllâh! You who pretend to read the Quran, you who pretend to understand the speech of the Lord, what more do you want me to say!? These are the words of the Lord, it is not me who invented all this!

If we took the Quran, you and me, and if we looked on what you could comprehend in it, we will constate that you do not even have *sadaqa Allâhu l-'adhîm!*[71] You do not have anything, absolutely anything! Not even a *madd* or a *sukûn* in the Quran... I swear by Allâh Almighty: you do not have it! The Quran has abandoned you, even before you abandoned it!

We affix on you the verse of the donkey carrying books, and we do that with the ultimate certainty (*haqq al-yaqîn*): **Those who were entrusted with the Torah and then did not take it on is like that of a donkey who carries volumes [of books]. Wretched is the example of the people who deny the signs of Allâh. And Allâh does not guide the wrongdoing people.**[72] As if this verse was not only about the people who were entrusted with the Torah, but including you who received the Quran.

It is why in the *lâm al-qabd*, I do not like... I could not stand to see any of you come and ask me stupid questions again: "why this... why that..."

The one who wants to sit, he can take a seat. As for the one who wants to leave, the doors are wide open! I have no more time to waste explaining secrets to you. When I say something, absorb it and if you cannot absorb it, stay home.

....

71 Allâh Most Mighty has told the truth.
72 Surat al-Jumu'a, verse 5.

They are some who come asking me questions… "Sidi Shaykh, should I go in this place or in this city or should I stay here?" Ask your heart! How many years spending to study here, and you still come and ask me such stupid questions? "Sidi Shaykh, should I attend the *mawlid*, or not?" Question your heart for God's sake!

Do you have the love of the Messenger of Allâh ﷺ or do you not have it!? If you do not have it, is it me who should forcefully drive it in your heart!? "I will go to work in Europe… but I will come back for the *Mawlid*." *SubhânAllâh*! Ignorance at its worst! You cannot do more…

He did the *khalwa*, he knew the *hâ'*, he understood the sense of **Indeed, those who pledge allegiance to you, they are actually pledging allegiance to Allâh.**[73] and he still dares to come and ask me "sidi Shaykh, should I stay or should I go?" With this question, do you even know what you are telling me!? You are telling me: "I did not study anything with you." or like if you are telling me: "I am still not sure yet: should I embrace Islam or not?" or like if you are clearly acknowledged that you do not know al-Mustafa ﷺ while you claim to have pledged allegiance to him.

Sell your properties and give everything to Allâh ﷺ, if you want to have the hope that He will be pleased with you! Follow the verse a little bit, what does it say? **Allâh has indeed purchased from the believers their lives and wealth in exchange for paradise.**[74]

By Allâh! If you do not sell your *nafs* and your properties, you will not enter it! If you do not sell your *nafs* and your

....

73   Surah al-Fath, verse 10.
74   Surah at-Tawbah, verse 111.

properties, by Allâh, you will not put even a foot! Unless the mercy of Allâh decides otherwise. But that is another matter.

All your protocols there, do not think that you are going for a job interview! Here, you go to present yourself to the Lord. In fact, if you could understand just a little bit, we will not need all these courses, all these explanations. We would get together, read the Quran, and that would be enough. If you could reach this certainty that He is closer to us that our own jugular vein and that He knows what our *nafs* are breathing into us, these courses would be absolutely no use, you would just have to burn them. Just understand these verses, and you will have understood everything.

But no, the carelessness (*al-ghafla*)—this amorphous dough that serves as your brain—this head full of sand... not one to rejoice my heart. Let each one question his own heart. I do not want to hear any more "that, I did not like... that secret, no really..." Thank Allâh for putting you where you are!

If we are having a look on your personal affairs, it would become clear that you are obviously not worthy of all this! Even myself, who am talking to you, if you are having a look into my own affairs, you would see for yourselves that I am not worthy of this. Then what to say of you, who had learned from me!?

Be as tired as you can, you will never be like me... and me, I have ruined myself...

If only, you would help
yourself to forget...

As human being, our Lord has breathed into us of His Spirit: **I blow in him of My spirit.**[75] So, we all have in us a breath, a Lord's insufflation. And in another verse: **Say, "The soul is of the affair of my Lord."**[76] so it is a Lord's order that you have! You have within your inner self a spiritual Breath or to speak bluntly: you have in your inner self the Spirit of the Lord ﷻ! From there, obviously this Spirit is perfectly disposed to rise and realize the ascent of the different spiritual degrees. Since it is the Spirit of the Creator, he cannot experience any difficulties to rise. In fact, it is rather you who have confined and imprisoned it. It is you who have prevented him from ascending and achieving spiritual ascension. You are therefore the punishment, you are the evil, you are what is execrable. As for the spirit, it is only purity, breath, *khuluq ar-Rahman*: it can only rise and return from where it came.

If only you would help yourself to forget yourself, to go beyond this state of confinement within yourself, you would access the absolute freedom. But when the disciple starts

....

75 Surah al-Hijr, verse 29.
76 Surah al-Isra, verse 85.

to make *dhikr*, he is unable to do that. As soon as he starts, he thinks about his children, if he is married with children or he thinks about his work, if he has a job or he thinks about his illness, if his body is sick and finds it difficult to devote himself to worship...

Regarding the one who is strong and healthy, he is absorbed and immersed in the admiration of his own strength. Whatever the situation, it is a problem. Whatever what you do... excepted the one to whom Allâh has shown mercy.

Thus, the spirit is perfectly disposed to ascend to the degrees from where he descended until into this body that Allâh ﷻ has modelled. But, why did He model it? Did He shape it and beautify it just like that? No, you are the one who think that. In fact, the Lord has shaped him in this way only so that he would be able to receive the Breath of the Spirit. He did not shape you to make you a model or something like that... no!

Our Lord shaped this body only to receive this Breath. And this spiritual could not have been received in any other body than yours! So, if you praise and thank your Lord for this bodily form of yours, then if you manage to forget about it and finally rise with the spirit, piercing the veils of appearances, until you return it to its original origin, He will make you ascend to the high spiritual stations, and you will embrace the divine and celestial Sciences. However, if you continue to imagine that this beauty and this strength are there just like that, by chance... then you will never understand the mystery of your being, the Secret of your existence, the elixir of your life: that for which you were created.

Look, Shaytân is in your pocket

Allâh ﷻ says: **There has certainly come to you a Messenger from among yourselves.**[77] but during all your life, you never look for the breath (*nafas*) of *sayiduna* al-Mustafa ﷺ while he is with you, he is in you! But you do not know it, you do not realize it, you do not want to connect to him. You prefer shift away from him. Our Lord, Him, is with us wherever we are. But us, we have never look for His Presence ﷻ.

What do we need? We need a body, a body which is for us a receptacle (*mustaqarr*) for this great news (*al-naba' al-'adhîm*), for this *nubuwa*, for this unknown domain (*ghayb*) but not a body like our body, which is just an animal body, which just need and seek to eat, to mate, to sleep. Such a being could not be considered as a Man, ever!

So restore your entity as the Creator conceived and shaped it initially. Be balanced, from the perfect balance of *sayiduna* al-Mustafa ﷺ. Love what the Prophet loves and hate what he hates. Eat what the Prophet eats. Sleep as the Prophet sleeps. Sit as the Prophet sits. Drink as the Prophet drinks. Travel as the Prophet travelled... that is how you will have actually shaped your body as you were asked, and then you will find *sayiduna* al-Mustafa ﷺ with you, accompanying you.

....

77 Surah at-Tawbah, verse 128.

You will constate that the Breath of the Merciful is flowing in you, from all eternity... and from then on, it will be possible for you to rise and achieve spiritual ascension (*ouroûj*).

SubhânAllâh, if your inner vision were open and if you opened the Book of the Lord to read in it the surah al-Kahf containing these deep meanings, containing what the Lord informs us about, you would be ashamed about yourself, you would be ashamed of your *shahâda*, your knowledge, your studies... You would realize that all this will have been a waste of time for you. A precious time that you will have lost... in nothing at all. Because if you had really been one of the students of Science, you would have understood the Message that was supposed to reach you.

Imagine yourself a little bit! You are living in the middle of a multitude of environments and peoples each one as different as the next and you did not even be able to know your own environment. In that time in which we live, you have reached the point where you do not even know your father and mother! All that, because of what technology, internet, and so on has brought you. You turned away of all intellect form, you do not resort anymore to the intellect nor to the vision nor to the meditation nor to the thoughts nor to the dhikr... you do not even read anymore! You do not study anything anymore! You just have two eyes which spend their time watching useless videos.

You do not do anything else except lose your time... at the point that you forget the link that you had with your parents, your wife, you family. You are with your mom or your father or your son in the same room but you are busy with something else, very busy, you are dived and completely plunged in another world, a world entirely built on the illusion. And it is you who will be able to transcend limits of this universe!? It is you who will be able to realize the spiritual ascension and bring us useful information for yourself and for us!? Completely impossible!

You are completely a waste of time. You do not have any existence. We only see you as a Caïn[78]: you killed your own soul, originally a pure spirit, you killed it! You killed it and you abandoned it in the *Tâghut*[79]...

If you are looking for where the *Shaytân*'s insufflations are and where they come from, it is very simple: in your pocket! When you take this little machine, this phone, know that these are only satanic insufflations. When you go on Google, you are in the middle of it. Understand that these insufflations have reached you in their lowest, closest, most concrete degree: the touch. The Shaytân has come down to you and has taken possession of your pocket, your intellect, the sense of touch of your hand.

If you could erase and disregard all this and return to a noble and elevated search (*'oluri*), in the domain of Faith. If instead of wasting your time in these trivialities, you would sit for a moment in the Presence of the Creator ﷻ, a sitting in which no one would come and mingle, a sitting that was pure and entirely dedicated to the Lord... not to ask something... only for His Proximity and the Proximity of the Prophet ﷺ.

....

78 Name of the son of the prophet Adam (*'alayhi salam*).
79 Variously interpreted to refer to idols, specific tyrant, oracle or opponent of the Prophet.

Then you could hope and pretend to reach those spiritual degrees we are talking about, you would become a being of the highest degree (*'olwi*) and in the morning you would inform us and tell us words that would turn heads and minds. You would bring us information, not imagined things, not invented stories! No, information from the *haqiqa*, based on the interpretation of noble verses. You would bring us these understandings and leave us all speechless. You would amaze us in the sunna, in the *fiqh*... you would be, yourself, the spirit of the religion. The spirit of the Quran.

Because the Quran, if it is deprived of its spirit... what is left of it?

Interrogate the great scholar
who is in you

If you have a fatwa to ask, there is a scholar who answers to all your questions. It is very accessible and very close to you: get up in the last third of the night. No one is telling you neither to do the *dhikr*, neither to pray, neither nothing at all. Just, do your ablutions and sit in front of the *qibla*. From there, ask the *fatwa* to your heart.

Question yourself.

It is him, the scholar who will never dupe you!

If you go to see someone else and tell him your story, he could answer you like your *nafs* will desire it but this scholar who is into you and to whom you ask in the middle of the night: "Who am I?" If you are a *shaytân*, by Allâh, he will tell you frankly! Despite all the artifices that you could execute during the day to prove the opposite! Your heart will give you an answer clear and irrevocably unless your conscience is dead.

The sign which indicates that the conscience of someone is dead, it is simply when he is unable to question his heart. Never. He is always running away from himself. As for the one whose the conscience is alive, he always calls himself to account. As *sayiduna* 'Omar ibn al-Khattâb (*radiAllâhu 'anhu*) tells us: "*Hold yourself accountable before you are held accountable.*"[80]

So, if you really are a Man... we are not even talking about a muslim, just a Man, a being with moral values of a Man in the same way that you assert yourself as such with your wife, your children, your neighbours... so be a Man with yourself at least once! Take a time, sit and question your heart. And when you will discover what is your *haqiqa*, go out and tell it to everyone.

Why should you be ashamed? If inside you, you are a *shaytân*, why are you pretending to be a *waliy*? That, it is the disaster... What will you do on the Day when you face your Lord?

He is telling you that He is closer to you that you own jugular vein but you, inside you, you reflect only the state of an eclipse! In your sky, there is no sun nor rain. And we do not know in that night, which is yours, why the rays of sunshine do not appear? So how can you, in the morning, become a *waliy* or even a *qotb*?

Me, you can mislead me, I can tell you that you are a *waliy*. On the contrary, in that there is a reward for me. From the moment I say good things about you, it is like if I were evoking Allâh. "So-and-so is one of the people of *al-Imân*" this is a *hasana* but what about you towards yourself?

Learn... learn to appreciate the taste of the pleading... I do not say to you to plead Allâh, obviously, you are not worthy of it, you do not reach the level to know how to plead Allâh.

....

80   Related by imam Ahmad.

But at least, talk, establish a dialogue with yourself it is very easy. Take a mirror… like the morning when you wake up and you contemplate yourself in the mirror, as usual, you fix your beard smiling… take this same mirror and talk to yourself.

Stop talking with people, talk to yourself: "Why did I do that? Why you do not want to be a good person!? Why I will not do that? Why I will not be like that?" You will see that the answer is in you because you have a scholar in your inner self… you have a *mufti*, you have al-Qardawiy in yourself and he answers to all your questions.

But you, no. You are unable of that. When you see yourself in the mirror, you like your reflection. You contemplate yourself. When you see a pimple you pop it, then you put some cream… and that's it.

In order to win,
break off from the group

When the children of *sayiduna* Ya'qub (*'alayhi salâm*) came to him and tell him: **Ô our father! Pray for the forgiveness of our sins. We have certainly been sinful. He said, "I will pray to my Lord for your forgiveness. He is indeed the All-Forgiving, Most Merciful."**[81]

Thus, he helped them by the invocations. His invocations were accepted because he was, himself, among the forgiven. He was among those about whom the True ﷻ said: *"When I love him, I am his hearing with which he hears, his sight with which he sees, his hand with which he strikes and his foot with which he walks. Were he to ask [something] of Me, I would surely give it to him."*[82]

And why does He answer him?

Because this servant is entirely dying out in His proximity. So why, you, sons of Ya'qub (*'alayhi salâm*), who are in the spiritual station of prophets, cannot call upon Allâh yourselves!? Because you got bogged down in the meanders of your *nafs* and your carelessness (*ghafla*) took a concrete apparent form, in the injustice you showed to your brother Yûsuf (*'alayhi salâm*).

....

81   Surah Yusuf, verses 97 and 98.
82   Hadith *qudsi* related by al-Bukhari.

Ô *murîd*, have you understood this?

They are guilty of injustice and they are guilty alongside the one who had the greater influence (*ta'hîr*) or the one who had the greater link established with the Lord in order to plead for them the Forgiveness.

But what does it mean here "*so that he may beg forgiveness for them*"? It means in order to help them to get out of the wavering of their *nafs* and the injustice with which they have burdened them. And what does *sayiduna* Ya'qub (*'alayhi salâm*) says to his sons when they came back to the city? He said: **O my sons, do not enter from one gate but enter from different gates.**[83] Why from different gates? Because when you gather together, it is a disaster! If you gather together, it will not be eleven prophets, rather it would be eleven *shaytân*! To avoid that then: split up!

Split up so that one does not have a negative impact on the other because as soon as you forgather...

The first time you have been forgather, you threw Yûsuf in the well! If you start again, if you enter all in the same door, you will set a new trap. So split up, stay separate, so that the flame of faith (*imân*) remains in you, pure.

And this is exactly the same thing that we are saying to the *murid*. Do not forgather to chat because as soon as you will forgather to chat, you will instigate traps against each other.

Let each one sit in his corner and beg for forgiveness from his Lord. Stop forgather to chat because it leads you inevitably on what sons of *sayiduna* Ya'qûb (*'alayhi salâm*) did. You begin with two then three... and as soon as you

....

83 Surah Yusuf, verse 67.

will be eleven, you will turn off the pre-eternal Sun. You will not turn on... you will turn off!

O my dear father! Indeed, I dreamt of eleven stars, and the sun, and the moon—I saw them prostrating to me![84] These eleven stars, there are those which turn off the pre-eternal Sun by throwing him at the back of the well, letting him open, hidden, at the back of a well, at the back of a cell during years until the Lord was willing, on schedule, to make him appear again. It is exactly the same for you.

As for the disciple... when does the great danger come? It is when the disciples forgather around him and design him as *muqaddam*. Because as soon as the *muqaddam* is designed, he will begin to make plans but his plans will always be according to what desire the *nafs* of disciples around him. If he had the misfortune to say to them something which go to the opposite of what their *nafs* want, obviously, he would be evicted and would lose his place whereas, him, what he wants, it is just to keep it. So, he will say and for that, he will do what disciples want... to let the group unite.

It is for this reason that when *sayiduna* Mûsa (*'alayhi salâm*) came back towards his people, he addressed directly to Hârun and took him by the beard because, he was afraid to talk to them directly too. If he addressed directly to them, the group would scatter. So, what could he do except tell them to stay there and adore the golden calf? He is careful with himself, obviously he will not adore the calf but in another part, the one who remain silent with something so serious... you know what it implies.

....

84 Surah Yusuf, verse 4.

Yourselves, you are talking about the fact to correct what is blameworthy (*al-munkar*) in accordance with the hadith, so forcibly or by the tongue and so on... is not it? So why you did not go toward Harûn (*'alayhi salam*) to slice his head!? It is the same thing for you, ô *murid*. The blameworthy (*al-munkar*), change it in yourself and focus on the link to establish with the one who will help you with his invocations.

Split up from the group of people in order to win what you have to win because the door, only one person will get through... not the group. It is in paradise that people will enter in groups. But the presence of the Lord, no. During the nightly ascent (*al-mi'râj*), the Prophet ﷺ went from door to door, until *sayiduna* Jibrîl (*'alayhi salâm*) told him, "*If you walk further, you will penetrate, but if I walk further, I will incinerate.*" That means, this passage can only be crossed alone. The door can only let one person through... not two.

And when he ﷺ met *sayiduna* Adam (*'alayhi salâm*), he did not say to him "come on let's go see *sayiduna* 'Issa in the second heaven... let's make *dhikr* together." No. He left alone and each of them stayed in their own station, with their own *wird*, in the presence of the Lord, period.

So, tell me, why do not you do the same thing in your side? Do not you aspire too to the ascent (*mi'raj*) of the spirit? Or is your *mi'râj* a jammed *mi'râj*? Are you going to enter with the caravan? Then stay with the caravan... you will only enter paradise and you will remain there in carelessness (*ghafla*).

The one who enter in the Lord's presence, at the Last Day (*yawm al-mazid*), he will enter it only alone. Each one will enter it alone and each one will find his own place, his own *kursi* where he will be able to install. And each one will drive to it and will talk to his Lord in private. This is in the *Sahîh* of al-Bukhâriy.

The Lord will not speak to you as a group. He will speak to each one of you individually. He will say to each one: "Do you remember that day when you did this and that...?" The servant will answer "Lord, have you not forgiven me?" and He will say "Yes, but only so that you will remember".

That means that He will speak to each of you according to his *maqam* depending what he reached and what he accomplished but you have to understand that the entry in the divine presence has to be done alone, not in a group! Alone because we are head for the One and the Exclusive.

The paradise, no, it is different. In the paradise, there are palaces, perfumes, all imaginable fruits and all the bird meats they want... and here you are, welcome to this huge market!

Here, it is clear: you will enter among people. You will visit, you will find a huge palace, you will ask to whom belong that and we will answer that it is the residence of so-and-so. And this one a little further, it is the residence of so-and-so. So, you will be in promenade like if you were in a car of tourists. "And what does he do to obtain such a palace?", "He did this and that...", "Oh, if only I had done what he did..." Is not it like in this lowly world, in the *dunia*?

However, the entry for the Lord's presence, that is done by itself. Here there is no palace, neither fruit, neither... Here is the extra day, the day of the Knowledge of the Lord. It is the day in addition to the normal days. And what is this day? It is the day of *jumu'a*[85]. It is the day where everybody will be reunite (*jumi'a*) in the paradise and where the privileged (*ahl al-ikhtisâs*) will access to the presence of the Lord... alone.

....
85   Friday.

The more you know the Shaykh,
the more you move away

Whatever you are doing for him... you will never be in measure to estimate the Shaykh to his fairly value. Why? Simply because you do not have the knowledge of the sanctify nature of his secret. Even if you live with him you entire life... you will never know the Shaykh.

Why will you never know the Shaykh?

Because you can only know from him the part that he assigned to you. You cannot know more than what he decided to show you of himself. You, he gave you a little bit but maybe to someone else, he gave more. And this one who received more than you, he is afraid of the Shaykh. It is impossible for him to sit with him. This is why you constate... who are those who sit a lot with the Shaykh? Who are those who laugh a lot with him? They are the news one, those who just arrived because they do not know the Shaykh. They do not know him, the things are normal for them: they enter: "oh sidi Shaykh, how are you? How is your health? ..." they start to tell stories and they constate that the Shaykh shows them some interest and he is open to the discussion then they turn and say: "oh the Shaykh, really, he is amazing, he is nice, pleasant, polite, gentle... he is a natural person, very accessible... he is very humble...".

But the one who received the secrets... does he can only approach him? It is not us who forbid him it, on the contrary! Rather, the sanctified secrets of the Shaykh have begun to reveal themselves to him, so he is afraid, he is even frightened, he melts in his presence. Because he realizes their greatness. He cannot get close to him. And the more the Shaykh reveals to him, the further away he gets!

With this in mind, the fact that he moves away does not mean that he separates himself from him! It is rather because this reverential fear (*khachia*) that is born in his heart, that he distances himself. He is afraid to speak, he is afraid to look, he is afraid to walk...

As for the other one... no, it is the opposite. Following the footsteps of the Shaykh... how does he understand it? He understands that when he walks, he must come behind the Shaykh and put his feet on the same spot where the Shaykh put his. This one acts exactly as al-Sâmiriy and he is not even aware of it. He says "I follow the footsteps of the Shaykh".

To follow the footsteps of the Shaykh is not to put your big shoes on his shoes, nor to have your shadow cover his shadow! To follow his footsteps, it is to observe him when he is walking and make this way he took as a way that you will take during your entire life. Here is what means "follow the Shaykh's footsteps"! Regarding his footsteps, you are not allowed to stamp them. Kiss them! Pass and kiss the footsteps of Allâh's people!

The sandals of *sayiduna* al-Mustafa ﷺ are embraced until today! Have you ever seen anyone daring to wear them on their feet!? We draw the *baraka* from the hair of the Prophet ﷺ by their sight alone or by touch, if you are one of the privileged ones. But no one would ever dare to put them on his head and mix them with his own hair! So, this is what *ta'dhîm* is.

The djellaba of the Prophet ﷺ, it is not there for someone to wear... no, it is a *baraka*. Due to the fact that it was worn by the close of the pact (*'ahd*) with the Lord, it became too close to the pact with the Lord, and that is why we seek its blessing.

The rules of *adab* differ and evolve according to the unveiling of the secrets because the *adab* is not a daily protocol that I must scrupulously observe. No. The protocol is done with kings, with presidents and ministers in order to achieve a specific goal. Here, no. There is no specific purpose or interest! Here, if you observe the propriety (*adab*), it is by obligation.

And be careful, it is not the Shaykh who made it mandatory. In no way. What made the *adab* mandatory, there are the secrets. It is the unveiling of this secret placed in your heart who obliged you to follow those rules.

The false modesty with the Shaykh

The Messenger of Allâh says: "*There are two types of people who never learn, the shy person and the arrogant person.*"[86]

Remember that and hang it with a nail in your brain. The shy one and the arrogant one.

The arrogant person will never learn… the one who imagines he is something, he stays and remains as the last one. He is intrinsically last because of his arrogance (*al-kibr*). It is a characteristic of the last one by excellence, the enemy of Allâh: Iblîs.

And the shy one… the one who does not dare whereas Allâh and His messenger ﷺ love the strong believer. And the strong believer, do not imagine that it is the one who picking up one tonne… No. It is the one who has an inner strength, the one who is confident in himself, sure about himself. He knows when he should feel shame. When to hush and when to talk to ask for advice something he needs.

"No, I have a question. Yes, indeed?" The Shaykh opens the door to ask but I do not want to talk. I am ashamed. So, I do the *adab*.". Okay, then stay in your place. The *adab* only comes to ask a question. As soon as the Shaykh leaves, you find yourself bellowing as a pop star! In this moment you forget about doing the *adab*!

....

86 Al-Bukhâriy.

Ask the question! Ask it with the *adab*! With this question, the one who listens to you will love you. If he understands you, he will answer you and if he does not understand then he will love you for the *adab* you have shown when asking. Because, there are those who we hope for... we wonder, "When will they speak?" and then there are others where we think when they will finally shut up!

There are those whose prayers are granted by the Lord, only to not have to listen to them talk anymore. They ask, over and over, until the Lord finally says "Give him what he asks for! Let him finally shut up!" because He does not like them. This is where you should understand that having your question or invocations answered is not the goal. The goal is only the knowledge (*ma'rifa*) of the Lord. If your Lord grants your wish but does not love you, then what have you won!?

And there are others who the Lord does not grant them their wishes. He loves to hear their invocations! He loves this servant, He loves his words!

As for you... you do not even talk! We have heard nothing from you, and you have not let us hear anything. As soon as we leave... that is it, your dynamo restart. You start blabbing! Here is the one who did not understand the meaning of "*adab*".

When *sayiduna* al-Khidr says to Musa (*'alayhi salâm*): **If you follow me, do not ask me about anything until I ask you to mention it.**[87] That means "Do not question me on subject that your intellect might not understand" but

....

87   Surah al-Kahf, verse 70.

obviously, as soon as we are together, as soon as we undertake a journey, it will necessarily for there to be questions and explanations about what we are doing on a daily basis. It is inevitable! "Are we going to sleep here?" "Are we going to eat?" "When are we going to sleep?" Clearly there will be conversations. However, as soon as I do or show you something that is beyond your ability to understand, do not ask me any questions about it! Do not ask for an explanation! Do not insist! Wait until the time comes for me to explain.

What does this mean, concretely, for the *murîd*? It means to never come and say, "Sidi Shaykh, give me the *idhn* to make *dhikr* with the name Allâh." As soon as I hear those words, I will instantly cut your water and electricity. If I hear, "Sidi Shaykh, let me enter to the *khalwa*," then you will never set a foot inside and you will never receive a secret. This is why al-Khidr says: **If you follow me, do not ask me about anything.** He does not mean questions like, "I have read such and such a verse and I think I have understood this and that. Is my understanding right?" The questions you need to avoid are the ones that show your impatience to hurry your journey in the Way. It is for example questions like "Sidi Shaykh, I have been in the *zawiya* for a long time, is not it time for you to bring me into the *khalwa*?" or "Give me the second secret!" or "Here is what I understood about the third secret." No. Even if you took the secret as laid it on my desk, you will never succeed. The secret has its rules, it has its station, it has its time when it can be expressed by the tongue.

Indeed, the Lord says: **In the rooms (hearts) where Allâh has allowed (*idhn*) to be raised and His name to be**

evoked therein.[88] until you receive this permission (*idhn*), and only after, can you devote yourself to *dhikr*. Here you learn to evoke (*dhikr*) the name of Allâh, accompanied by the vision of the attribute of Allâh, in order to reach the essence of Allâh.

This is what you do not have the right to talk about until the *idhn* of Allâh comes to you. If you talk about it, you certainly show a lack of *adab*. However, for the tasks you go through daily it is your absolute right to express yourself. Frame your question within the boundaries of the *adab*. If you refuse to ask, you will not learn anything. It is as simple as that.

If you never ask, then you will learn only through questions of other people. And here, you will need to be smart and perceptive. It is the smart and perceptive ones who learns not only from the signs which are sent to him but also from those sent to others. As for the idiot, he does not understand signs that were sent to him. How can he understand what concerns others!?

But you, you confuse insight with trickery. The ones we qualify as smart and perceptive, you understand as him knowing plenty of dirty tricks. No! Do not confuse the part that is perceptive with the other part of the dirty tricks. Do not mix up them.

....

88   Surah an-Nur, verse 36.

Never underestimate the importance
of the intermediary

This darkness… When will you know their reality?

I answer to you through a simple exercise. When you finish your adorations, you go to your bedroom to sleep. You turn off the light and you see the light pin you down from everywhere. Do not close your eyes. Open them without focusing on the center or on the *qibla* like it was the case with your *bay'a*. Let your eyes come and go in the darkness. The first thing to happen is a state of oppression (*qabd*) then the fear then the terror. You cannot continue like that for long and you hope for only one thing. That sleep comes as soon as possible. Some people, during the day, enjoy acting tough. They pretend that no matter what the circumstance or the danger, they will face it without shuddering. But after diving into the darkness, they are not able to take a single step.

The Shaykh takes you from the middle of this darkness and he makes you see the light of the heavens and the earth. You enter in this light, which is like a scarlet rose, and begin the link. At this point you enjoy being alone in the dark, staying only with the light of the Lord.

Then, you do not even feel any fear regarding this darkness. You begin to search in this light of existence and you see in it what is in heavens and earth. Then, you imagine that you seize the entire knowledge (*ma'rifa*), to get all what you have to understand and to see all what you have to see. However, if we make you see what is in the darkness, you would have known that it was quite different from what you imagined it to be in the beginning, namely nothing at all, total nothingness.

You would know that this nil has an existence due to the One who let this nil enter the existence. This nil that you consider pure nil is, in fact, made up of a multitude of existing things.

What are these things, what are these spirits, what are these characteristics, what are these knowledges, what are these sciences that you will find in the darkness, but you will not find in the light? To put it simply, I will popularize things in a concrete example. In the darkness, if someone comes to kill himself – and how many people are doing that today – or if someone finishes committing the adultery or a sin among the biggest sins, someone who would be destined to the fire of the hell, this person, in the darkness of the hereafter, he will not stop to reproduce the same act.

However, during your *siyaha* in and through the divine light, you will meet angels, prophets and messengers, saints, letters, names and you will go from experience to experience, never ceasing to rise through them. In the darkness, the one who killed himself will not cease from reproducing this act and will kill himself over and over. He will not talk, not a word. His only expressions will be those of its look, who will transmit the feeling of a perpetual terror. When he will look around him, he will see people who are in a state worse that his and it will console him, and it will prevent him to leave this infernal loop.

This darkness is in reality full. They are not empty. And their breath has a direct influence on you when you fall asleep. The breath, it means the breath of the acts of those who swim in the ocean of darkness, those who are so drown in it as they cannot see themselves... how could you see them, you? Their simple breath transmits to you this state of oppression (*qabd*) and of pain in the heart.

Realize the value of this intermediary (*wasita*) who came to take you among them. He lets you swim in their ocean that he splits it in half. He made the star appear to you and sent it into your heart. He took you from the midst of oppression (*qabd*), fear, terror... and he made appear in you the beauty (*jamâl*) and the love. At the point you were not scared of anything. You have been comforted with an eternal comfort through the company of your Lord while there are some who are unable to sleep in the dark and must constantly leave a light on.

This is what you hear especially from those who followed a Shaykh who was not a real Shaykh, a Shaykh who told them to devote themselves to the *dhikr* of a name among the names of Allâh... al-Lateef[89] or al-Qawiy[90] or al-Samî'[91] or even the Name Allâh!

The disciple began the practice of this *dhikr* assiduously but obviously, the darkness is filled so what do you think he could see? It was not the spirits of darkness that came out and threw themselves upon him, but it is himself who plunged into their world! He swam in their ocean and saw

....

89   The Subtle One, The Most Gentle.
90   The All-Strong.
91   The All-Hearing.

what filled his heart with dread. This is how this pathfinder ended up going completely crazy and lost all reason. He is not even able to perform *dhikr* or worship anymore. If he starts to pray, for example, his heart is immediately overwhelmed by an unbearable terror. There are so many such examples. This is the value and importance of the intermediary (*wâsita*). Never underestimate him!

If he wanted you to get lost, he would lose you. It is simple for him. In the same way, he lets you see the light, he can give you the eclipse and leave you alone with your own issues. You will constate then that you are afraid of yourself. At least, you will receive a true education (*tarbiya*).

Take care to always keep the right opinion and cultivate a virtuous intention, thus you will advance on the Path of the Prophet ﷺ. And if you have fed a bad opinion of your Shaykh, know that he never had a bad opinion of you. He left you as you are, without ever making you see what is in that darkness.

If he had done it... if he had shown you even a part of what is in the darkness... of all that you have seen in the light, you must know that the exact same thing is found on the other side, in the darkness. If you had seen even an image of that darkness, you would have been looking for death before your time.

So, it is absolutely necessary and essential for everyone in this Way to change his intention to a positive... as long as you still have time. That means, before the veil is lifted for him and he knows the *jalâl*... We called it *jalâl* but in fact, they are just spirits and terrifying creatures. If you saw them, you will forget your past, your present and your future. You will even forget who you are, the horror would be so great.

To learn a little about this fear, we tell you to sit in a dark room and begin to scan this darkness. Not with the spiritual strength of your Shaykh in order to detect the light like during your *bay'a* but simply with the intention to see what is in this darkness, you will taste the *qabd* in the obscurity.

However, you have to know that if you were to get lost, you could never come back. Exactly like the one who truly tastes the light and get lost, he will never come back.

Be part of the people of the light

It does not fit a human being to whom Allâh gave the privilege (*khoussoûssiya*) to tell people: **Be devoted to the worship of your Lord alone.**[92] This being, Allâh elected him and gave him privileges among everybody. He projected in his heart His Light and made him a torch for all communities of men. He brings the believer out from darkness into the light! Just this verse... if you become aware, it would leave you frozen!

Allâh is the Waliy of those who believe. He brings them out from darkness into the light.[93]

Learn to know **Allâh is the Waliy.** The *waliy* being the servant (*'abid*), understand that this *wilaya* of Allâh has manifested itself to you through the servant and the proof of the authenticity of that is the coming out of darkness into the Light.

With this in mind, He brings the believer (*mu'min*) out from darkness into the Light. The *mu'min*... so if you are muslim, you do not have any part into the Light. The *waliy* is a messenger sent to the people of the degree of *al-Imân*. He is not the Messenger ﷺ who is send for the whole universe. The *waliy* is reserved for the *mu'min*. And those

....

92   Surah al-'Imran, verse 79.
93   Surah al-Baqarah, verse 257.

believers (*mu'min*), they are initially in the darkness and they remain in it until the *waliy* comes and lets them out.

The believers are indeed believers, they believe in Allâh, in His angels, in His books, in His messengers, in the Last Day, in the destiny good or bad but they do not see the Light until the *waliy* came to them and brought them out from darkness into the Light.

Allâh is the Waliy. If you can get what these words mean... **Allâh is the Waliy of those who believe. He brings them out from darkness into the light.** This is really a privilege which is reserved only to those of the degree of *al-Imân*. The verse does not say: "Allâh is the *waliy* of those who are muslims"!

The bedouin said: "We have believed." Say, "You have not believed"; but say "We have submitted (*aslamna*), for faith (*Imân*) has not yet entered your hearts."[94] You do not have *al-Imân*, you just have *al-Islâm* until *al-Imân* penetrate into your heart.

So, *al-Imân* entered in the heart of the muslim, making him a *mu'min* but does this *mu'min* see the Light of Allâh? No, until the *waliy* comes to bring him out of the darkness into the Light. As long as he did not meet the *waliy* to let him out from darkness into the Light, he is not considered as part of people of the Light. And indeed, he met the *waliy,* but he did not want to go out from darkness into the Light because this person has already his program in his head, how things are and how they should happen. Let him begin by deleting his program. Do not say that you deleted it or that you will delete it. Delete it!

....

94   Surah al-Hujurat, verse 14.

Here, words are useless. Words, it is for the others *zawiya*. There, indeed, talk, show yourself off. Here, no: erase yourself, disappear. You do not have anything to say here. Here, instead of talking, work, provide something! Provide and only after, express yourself.

As long as you did not produce anything, you do not have to talk because you do not even realize the first pillar of Islam. Realize the *shahâda* then realize the establishment of this link (*silat*), then realize the purification (*tazkiya*) of the *nafs* then realize the *samdâniya* through the *khalwa* of forty days and forty nights and then the Hajj.

If you do not have any of that: silence, hush!

Because at each word that you pronounce, the Shaykh stamps you. You, you talk and the Shaykh follows you and stamps all things that you say. And be careful, the Shaykh does not forget! He can forget things who concern him but what is concerning you, no, he does not forget them! And from there, he lets you see your reality step by step. The Shaykh assembles your files day after day... When you talk, he slaps you by answering you with your own answer, with what you pronounce yourself with your mouth. He does not talk with you with his words. No, the Shaykh talk to you by and with your tongue!

He lets you enter to the *khalwa* by your own spiritual aspiration (*himma*)! It makes you see reality as you should see it, you! Regarding the fact that he gives you what he has in him, start by discovering and knowing who you are, you! Then, only, learn to know him. But do not play with pronouns whereas you do not even know yourself.

Forgot people around you

Allâh says: **And build the Ark under Our Eyes and directions, and do not plead with Me for those who have done wrong, for they will surely be drowned.**[95]

The story of *sayiduna* Nûh (*'alayhi salâm*) is really extraordinary... Imagine, a man who goes to the middle of the desert where there is no water. He goes to the top of the higher mountain and built a boat. You, when you tell these qoranic stories to your children or your brothers, you claim, full of condescension: "Haha, his son refused to follow him! He did not follow him, his son is a miscreant... haha...".

You who is laughing, if you had been his son, you would have killed him for sure! If your father was gone in the middle of the desert, on the mountain and built a boat, you want to make us believe that you, you would have faith on him!? Come on, you who teach the story to others... let us see.

Obviously, since it is the Quran that mentions it, you believe in it. And you ask yourself why this son did not believe his father but if your own father would have been the same thing, you would have asked to yourself: "Is it truly a revelation of Allâh or just a new philosophy that got into his head and made him think that this is it, he has reached this spiritual degree?"

....

95   Surah Hud, verse 37.

So, try to replace things is their contexts and to understand them in their deep realities. It is for this reason that the Lord says: **Build the Ark under Our Eyes,** what does it mean **under Our Eyes?** That means do not move, do not do the slightest move without having received the sign beforehand. If you reach for that then, indeed, you would have been reaching this *maqam* and you would become from those who evolve under Lord's eyes ﷻ.

Because in the hadith *qudsi*: "*The servant does not draw near to Me with anything more loved to Me than the religious duties I have obligated upon him. And My servant continues to draw near to me with nafil (supererogatory) deeds until I Love him. When I Love him, I am his hearing with which he hears, and his sight with which he SEES...*"[96] From there, understand that it is not about interpreting the message (*risala*) as you wish and putting it into practice. It is valid only because your sight become the sight of the True ﷻ!

But us, no... how we proceed: This thing pleases us... yes, the Messenger of Allâh ﷺ did it! This other thing does not please us... we flee in the *ijtihad*. "It is allowed in the Shafi'i or in the Hanafi..." and so we interpret things as we please. No, rather, you have to search what will dawn in you a strength of *Imân* even if you have to go against all your people to not conflict and to conform to a divine sign. See to what level of magnification (*ta'dhim*) of the *ichâra* does it correspond!

Consider when *sayiduna* Ibrahim ('*alayhi salâm*) see that he had to behead his son... in dream! And you, if you dreamed that you have to behead your son, could you, do

....

96   Hadith *qudsi* related by al-Bukhari.

it? Basically, you do not even have the certainty regarding the nature of what you see: was it a pious dream (*ro'ya*) or an insufflation from Shaytân?

So, you see that the problem is not in the fact that your son refuses to obey you, the problem, it is also with the person who dreamed. Do you sleep truly in a state of Lord's contemplation or rather on Shaytân's insufflations?

Consider yourself only, do not see anyone else. Forget people and search in yourself before to meet the Lord! The other, he will be judged according to his nature, according to his spiritual degree, according to the degree of his intellect, according to the strength of his *Imân* but for you too, it is the same thing! Then see what you seized, what you understood of that! And stop interpretating the *risâla* or the *naba'* as you want. Do not act only if the clear sign would reach you and you would magnify it and estimated to its true value.

Because you, you have the *ichara* but you are not even convinced by it. This is the problem! Every day, you see Lights, you see divines Names, you see koranic verses, letters and so on... but you do not trust at all what you are seeing! Not that what you are seeing is false, no... rather the mistake is in you! It is you who did not reach yet this degree of strength in the *Imân*.

The *'arif* based himself on the obvious proof (*bayina*) of his Lord and he does not act except by and in accordance with a sign (*ichara*) which would reach him from his Lord. Even if the entire world makes fun of him and ridicules him. He does not despair, and he does not let it afflict him. You have the certainty and you are absolutely convinced by the *muraqa'a*, there are even people who see the Messenger of

Allâh wearing a *muraqa'a*. From an apparent and exoteric point of view, the one who wore it, it is *sayiduna* 'Omar ibn al-Khattâb but some people received an *ichara* of their Lord stronger than that.

If you really have the certainty (*yaqin*), people can make fun of you as much as they like, what does it matter to me, as long as I am convinced of what I am doing? *Sayiduna* Nûh too, people make fun of him. Those who followed him were very few, a handful of people, and among the weakest, most despised... as well as those who supported the Messenger of Allâh 🕌 were the most despised of the people of the time.

So, meditate to the sense of the koranic expression: "under Our eyes". You, you see the Light of Allâh and when some people describe the supreme examples of the manifestation of this Light namely that the niche, the lamp, the crystal, the star of great brilliance, they say "It is like if I see an eye..." but you never said... you never through... it never brushes your spirit that it can be the Eye of the True 🕌!

Since He says: **Allâh is the Light of the heavens and the earth. His light is like a niche in which there is a lamp, the lamp is in a crystal, the crystal is like a shining star.**[97]

If you were to draw this on a board, would it look like an eye? Obviously, this is not an eye. So, if you named it the eye of the heart, no problem... only for some people, the strength of *Imân* has reached such a degree that they said that this is the Eye of the True 🕌.

You protest by claiming that it is an ignominy and an uttered lie towards Allâh but come back to the story of

....

97   Surah an-Nur, verse 35.

sayiduna Ibrahim (*'alayhi salâm*) when he saw a star. What did he say? He did not say "Here is a Star!" but **Here is my Lord!**[98], referring to his degree of certainty (*yaqîn*) and the importance (*ta'dhîm*) he attached to it. So, what are you going to say? That *sayiduna* Ibrahim was miscreant?

Astaghfirullâh... Sayiduna Ibrahim (*'alayhi salâm*), as well as all the prophets and messengers: it is impossible for them to fall in the *kufr* or the ignominy, it is the opposite, they are infallible. So, when he saw the star, he said **Here is my Lord!** because it was an *ichâra* coming from the Lord. Then, when he saw the Sun: **Here is my Lord, this one is bigger!**[99]

All that show the *ta'dhîm* of the *ichara* and it is through the *ta'dhîm*, through magnifying the signs of his Lord, that he could finally reach: **I have turned my face toward He who created the heavens and the earth, inclining toward truth, and I am not of those who associate others with Allâh.**[100]

If he had not first had the *ta'dhîm* for the Star, he would never have been able to reach the vision of the Moon, nor that of the Sun. Thanks to the *ta'dhîm*, the different degrees of theophany were revealed to him one after the other until he reached and realized the state of Presence, directing himself and resigning himself entirely to the Original *Qibla*.

....

98   Surah al-Anam, verse 76.
99   Surah al-Anam, verse 78.
100 Surah al-Anam, verse 79.

Your behaviour describes
your inner state

If you constate that in your heart there is heaviness in the accomplishment of the adorations, a heaviness of the accomplishment of your *wird*, of the prayer or of the fast so know that you must return to the study of the reality of your heart and you must return to the supplication of the Divine Forgiveness (*istighfâr*) so that your troubles may fade away and the rust that has affected your heart may disappear. Because if you had truly tasted the taste of worship, the veil would have been lifted from you.

Do not pretend to be from those who's the veil has been lifted whereas you are being lazy in your adorations! Those for who the veil has been lifted, they are always the first in the adoration of the Lord ﷻ. This mystical experience of the unveiling is an experience accessible by the certainty (*yaqin*) by the Love and by the assertive and definitive establishment of the heart's mirror after he has been duly polished and stripped of all his inclinations towards the trivia of this world. Because like *sayiduna* al-Mustafa ﷺ teaches us, the hearts rust like the iron when it is touch by the water and it is by the *dhikr* of Allâh that we polish them.

Why by the *dhikr* of Allâh? Simply because the reason of the rust of the hearts, it is their carelessness. The absence of the *dhikr* lead to the carelessness and the inclination towards the passions of the *nafs* so a state of distancing. There are some of them for whom the sitting of *dhikr* is heavy.

What does it mean? That your heart is rusted! Even if you would come tell us that you see moon and stars, that you have wonderful and amazing visions, we cannot believe you, you are not reliable because when you are sitting with us, you are not present.

It is the body which translate the state of the heart. Your tongue, your members... If your tongue is carefree and if your members are carefree... stop lying to yourself, stop saying "Me I, me I, me I..." Impossible!

If your inner state was really what you claim it to be, it would have manifested itself in an apparent way on your body. It is like if your inner self or your heart, were a book who's your outer body would be the cover. The title of this book, it is you.

As *sayiduna* 'Ali says: "If the *'arif* speaks, we identify him within the hour. And if he does not speak, we identify him within the day" because your tongue reveals everything about you so that when you express yourself, you are not expressing anything other than what is in you. Even if you give examples for others, you are not really touching anyone but your own heart.

If an eminently elevated and heavenly word spreads from you then know that your heart has indeed pierced the veil. And on the contrary, if your word is vile and shameful, know that you are entangled and submerged in darkness. The words you use to express yourself, even if they are not necessarily of a high degree in the Arabic language, they are still words full of *Imân*, full of *adab*, *khushû'*, appeasement, tranquillity... such is the language of the believer.

On the contrary, your tongue is only laughter, fun and obscenities then it is impossible for us to tell you that you have a heart controlled and strongly established in the divine Presence.

The goal is Allâh

We do not say to people from other ways that they are
in the bewilderment. Their affair concerns them, it is
between them and Allâh and it is returning to the intention
that each one have in his heart. We do not say that we are
the best but when we talk to you about the Light, what we
are saying, it is: "Allâh ﷻ said", and "The Messenger of
Allâh ﷺ said".

May you understand or not, it is the same. When you
close your eyes, you see the Light and you see it mentioned
in the Quran. Among the most beautiful Names of Allâh:
an-Nûr (The Light). Among the surahs of the Quran, surah
an-Nûr. Not less than thirty-six verses mentioning the Light
including twelve in the degree of the Islam, twelve in the
degree of the *Imân* and twelve in the degree of the *Ihsân*.
And if you imagine that the Lord will come down to you
with a big beard, know that the Lord is incomparable and
could not be associated to what you imagine! Wake up, ô
reckless!

And if you do not have more ambition than to enter the
highest degree of the paradise (*al-Firdaws*), know that the
Lord is able for so much more! But this is not His goal.

The Goal, it is the owner of the home, not the home
itself! You, for example, you come to the *zawiya*, you eat,
you drink but if I left, your presence here would be mean-
ingless. Not because you will lack food or pillow to sleep,

no, on the contrary we will give you better pillow that those one and cooked dishes more tasting that those one, you would find people with whom you would get along better than those who are here but if you have come all the way here, it is with a precise goal: it is with an intention that you have placed in the Shaykh in order to come and talk to him and benefit from him directly. The day the Shaykh will tell you that he is leaving on a *siyâha*, that he will say good-bye to everyone and farewell... three days after leaving I will not find anyone here.

Understand if you have the capacity to understand!

The paradise... enter in it and enjoy these pleasures until to be tired! But when the Lord will welcome people who have more (*al-mazid*), people of the Throne of the Merciful... you no, stay here and eat your apple! Eat a whole crate even!

The Muslims, we do not say for none of them that they will enter the Fire. If Muslims go to Hell, who will go to Heaven? Jews and Christians maybe? Muslims are all in paradise! So, if your goal is nothing more than paradise, go ahead, you are already there!

As the Messenger of Allâh ﷺ told us: fast one month in a year, pray your five prayers, pay *zakat*, make Hajj once in your life and you are guaranteed to enter paradise. It is not me who say that but the Prophet ﷺ. Do not stay here in the *zawiya* any longer: if this is your goal, then go and live your life. You think we are here to fight for paradise? No, you are mistaken. What we want, it is to understand! Understand the link between the servitude and the seigneury. We want to know the Word of the Lord. We want the total extinction and the evanescence (*fana*).

Regarding the fact to do the dhikr to build palaces in paradise, if we want that, it is only because the paradise is the access door of the divine Presence because if there was another door, we will present ourselves.

The paradise is a step, a waiting room before to be able to reach the Lord. And we fear that while people will enter in the presence of the Lord, you, you remain waiting in the waiting room as vast as it is. If the goal of the messenger of Allâh ﷺ would have been the paradise, he would cross the heavens. Why would he have risen to *al-Muntaha*? For what? Why not just meet *sayiduna* Adam (*'alayhi salâm*) and even the intimate Ibrahim (*'alayhi salâm*) then turn around and go back?

Where are you going, ô Messenger of Allâh ﷺ?

Look what is the goal of the Prophet ﷺ. The paradise is not the objective of the Messenger ﷺ, no! Look carefully, when *sayiduna* Jibril said to him: "*Would the intimate friend leave his companion this way?*" because his goal is not in *sayiduna* Jibril (*'alayhi salam*).

If it was the case, he would stay with him, he would be unable to break off from him "If you cannot cross then me neither I cannot, I stay with my intimate friend. I stay with the one who brought me the Quran, the one who made shining the Light of my heart, the one who made me discover the reality of things, the one who made me discover the degree of paradise and hell. I stay with him, why would I break off from him?

But no! Because my first goal, it is to cross, it is to burn and to consume myself, it is the state of the ultimate presence, it is the entry of *al-Muntaha* who does not accept any duality. You will not find in it neither sidi Ahmed al-Rifa'i, nor sidi AbdelQader al-Jilani! No, rather, you will find in it anyone else except the Lord of sidi Ahmed al-Rifa'i and sidi AbdelQader al-Jilani!

This is the Goal! You and Allâh.

It is what I want, and it is what the Prophet ﷺ says. If I had wanted heaven and these things, I would have been satisfied with the first heaven. There I would have found on the right of Adam (*'alayhi salâm*), all the people of paradise and on his left all the people of Hell. I would have seen the place of so-and-so and then I would have returned to my daily life.

But no, he wanted *al-Muntaha*, he wanted the infinity and absolute, he wanted to see beyond the horizon, beyond all the limits. This is why he burnt out, melted and disappear completely until to say: "You are as You described Yourself". This is a word, a *tafsir*, a wisdom, a hadith, a sign which remain alive for the eternity. Is this exclusively reserved to the Prophet ﷺ or also for other people?

Alhamdulillah, we have a Messenger ﷺ such as no man could be compared to him, both in mercy, affection and love because he lets enter in it all the virtuous (*salihin*) saying: *as-salâmu 'alayna wa 'ala 'ibâdiLlâhi s-Sâlihîn.*[101] This is why we are looking for the Virtue (*as-salâh*): it is to access to *al-Muntaha*, not to enter in the paradise! The one who wants the paradise, the paradise is not in the *zawiya*. May him go away, far from us! At the moment where he is part of the *umma* of *sayiduna* al-Musafa ﷺ, the paradise, he is already in it. The one who wants palaces, may Allâh give him more than that!

....

101 May the peace be upon us as well as upon the virtuous servants of Allâh.

Regarding the one who wants the Light, welcome to him here, because it is exactly for that that we reunite here. And if he imagines that he will go in another place and find him the Light of the Lord, he will see that we already outstripped him, and we are already in it! Because it is impossible for us to know that there is Light in somewhere without going in it. Impossible! This is the Truth.

If the paradise is what you have in the heart, you are already in it so why are bothered to pray and stay awake all the night? Settle for your five prayers by day and then go, let me have some place. It does not go any further than that without feeding doubts about me or me about yourself and without having to zigzag in your consideration of the Light of the Lord: is it the Truth or what ignorant said about it.

Let the divine Light to people of Light, to people of the Presence! This is the reality.

The Messenger of Allâh ﷺ stays bow down and he says to people to pass, to enter to the paradise! He is the free pass of the whole *umma*. Then enter the Prophets and the Messengers. Then finally the sinners, whom he saves from the Fire and brings into paradise, and he is the last one to enter paradise... It is him the key who open and close the door of the paradise ﷺ. After him, no one enter anymore. And he hopes, he would not like to bring the whole world into it but THE worlds because it is him who was sent as a mercy for the worlds.

But you, in your preconceived idea, you imagine that the Messenger of Allâh ﷺ is installed in the middle of the paradise and he will make you come to him whereas no! He is not a Shaykh. He is not a Shaykh or an Imam who will make you come to him so that you pray in the front rank behind him... no. The Messenger of Allâh ﷺ, he is the one who teach you the humility or rather the humiliation and the belittlement at the lowest degree which exist. He is the one to whom we broke a tooth, he is the one who has been hit, he is the one on whom we throwed trash etc.

You, no one broke your teeth, no one hit you, you do not even accept the fact to be belittled to learn, you do not even have an atom of acts of the Messenger of Allâh ﷺ.

You are relying on what is commonly admitted and because you heard one or two passages of the *sira*, you imagine that the Messenger of Allâh is comfortably sitting in the paradise, and he calls people to come with him... but no! In fact, the Messenger of Allâh took and supported the hits to teach you and to permit you to enter but him, he was already in it. He was already in it and to let you see it too, watch how many canings he took! He was at *al-Muntaha,* and he came down...

In the hadith: "*The first thing Allâh created is the Light of your prophet ô Jabir.*" So, he came down and manifested himself, in the form of *sayiduna* Muhammad ibn 'Abdillah to let you reach the words that your understanding would be able to seize... as for him, it is enough for him to be just the original Light without having to come down and to belittle in an apparent and human form. Thus, he belittled to let you see a human like you and to let you be able to understand what should be understandable. Today, you consider about your narrow consideration that the sunna of the Messenger of Allâh ﷺ it is what he said, what he did and what he confirmed and if we removed the texts saying that he is in fact the Light maybe you will even deny the Truth! Yet, it is really that his *haqiqa*! This is this Light that you are seeing! This Light that you are seeing, it is the prophet. So go read *al-Jawahir* of ibn 'Ajiba who talk about it very clearly...

Knowing that you do not give importance to this Light, we are saying to you that it is the Star of *sayiduna* al-Musafa ﷺ but in fact, it is him! The messenger of Allâh. His essence, his attributes, people of his house, his Quran, his Sunna, it is this Star, whether you like it or not.

And if you, you do not accept it, us, we are imploring Allâh to preserve us under his footsteps and his traces for the eternity.

You have more than one name,
find them

Sayiduna al-Mustafa ﷺ said in a hadith: "*The first thing Allâh created, it is the Light of your prophet, ô Jabir.*" The Light of your prophet... look, it is like if he has been prophet only for Jabir because he ﷺ did not say: "It is the Light of your Prophet to all of you, ô Jabir". He did not say neither: "It is the Light of the Prophet". That means that the prophet came for you, ô Jabir, in the form and the characteristics that you seized and understood. Regarding the others: *Muhammadun Rassoûlullâh*. Muhammad on the Earth and Ahmed in the sky. Yet, the highest names are not those that we use on the Earth. What do you know about *sayiduna* al-Mustafa ﷺ?

You know Muhammad who walk on the Earth. You know the Messenger on the Earth. But now, share with us his ahmadian biography then, when you will finish, bring us something about the biography of Ya-Sîn. Bring us the biography of Ta-Hâ. Ô you who pretend to know the *sirâ*... where are you?

The messenger of Allâh ﷺ does not have just a name. What do you know about him? You read three or four hadiths and that is it, you pretend to know him... "The messenger of Allâh said *bismiLlâh* before to begin to eat", yes, but here you only see his human form. Explain us the meaning of the names that the True used to name him, why did He call him Ta-Hâ? Why Abul-Qâssim? Why all these names?

You too, ô man, you imagine that you have only one name and when we questioned you on this topic, you answer that your name is so-and-so. But tell me, what is your name in the first sky, in the second, in the third, the fourth, the fifth...? In fact, you do not even know your own *sira*. You ignore until your own person! Who are you? What are your names?

We do not talk here on what concern you, personally, know that if you were knew on the Earth under the name of 'Abbâs, the residents of the sky do not know you because they do not know 'Abbâs, they only know your name in the sky. If you reach the knowledge of these esoteric links between things, you will seize the noble names which are you owns.

If we evoke all that, it is simply to let you understand what the news contains (*al-naba'*) to let you have an idea about the Science of *al-naba'*. In that sense, we bring the verse referring to *sayiduna* Adam (*'alayhi salam*) because it is about him that the book of Allâh informs us clearly and explicitly that he received this Science: **He taught Adam the names of all things.**"[102]

Considering that the name "Allâh" is the name which reunited them all, the indicator Name of the divine Essence, it simply means that *sayiduna* Adam (*'alayhi salam*) received the Science of this Name. Henceforth, it is up to you to

....

102 Surah al-Baqarah, verse 31.

endeavour and to look for what is your name in the first sky and I prevent you in advance: do not wait to be informed by the intermediary of a dream or a *mushâhada* whereupon you will say: "I perceived a *hâtif* who tell me that my name was so-and-so..." False! Or "I slept, and I saw in a dream that my name in the sky was so-and-so..." False!

Your name is the product arisen from all your being, from the strength of your Faith's degrees. He must appear as the name dominating the name which is yours in the *Mulk*. Then you will discover that this name is your Source and if you could dive and immerge completely in this Source, it will lead you to the even deeper Source. As well as in your pathway through the name "Allâh": your immersion and you're diving in the *hâ'* leads you to the *lam* then to the *lam* then to the *fasl* then to the *wasl* then to the *alif al-muqaddar*.

Thus, diving into your name will lead you to the name of your name then to the name of the name of your name then to the name of the name of the name of your name until to reach the name which will reunite them all. You will discover that this is just an only name, intrinsically linked to all the other names and you will learn how from this fundamental name, come down in the whole of his branched names until returning to your name. It is at this moment that you will truly know all things that concern you.

This is the real meaning of "*Fear the farsightedness vision (firâsa) of the believer, for he sees by the Light of Allâh.*"[103] The *firasa*, the farsightedness vision of the believer, it is not

....

103 al-Tirmidhî.

what people reduce it nowadays… "You have black eyes that means this and that… if you had blue eyes, it would have meant this and that…"

No, the true *firasa* of Faith's people, it is an esoteric flow beginning from a name to another name, to another name… to a name which reunited them all. Then, the descent from a name to another name to another name… until returning to the first name considered and then you perceive what is his character, what are his noble states and his bad states. At this moment, you would seize from him the whole of your person in a simple fraction of second only if you are among those who restrain the ascension (*'ourouj*) and the descent (*nouzoul*).

This is what *sayiduna* al-Mustafa ﷺ realized: He soared and went down, soared and went down, soared and went down… five times consecutively until the *sidrat al-muntaha* where he brings us the prayer with the specific gestures and the result of that, it is that you, you just have to pray and you enjoy the beneficial of this ascension like if you have prayed at *sidrat al-muntaha* according to the degree and the strength of your faith and your sincerity of the following of the prophet ﷺ.

You have a name
between names of Allâh

Allâh ❈ says: **Allâh has already set for everything a [decreed] extent (*qadar*).**[104] This *qaddar* that Allâh ❈ established, it is the intrinsic beauty of everything. We do not talk about the beauty (*jamal*) of the apparent form but the original beauty of the thing. Knowing that each thing is considering according to his luminous degree (*martabat al-nurâniya*) and not according to his apparent form.

When the person watches things in their physical dimension, apparent and material, what he thinks to perceive of the beauty (*jamâl*) has, in fact, nothing intrinsically beautiful. Because the Lord ❈ says: **Everyone upon it will perish, and there will remain the Face of your Lord, Owner of Majesty and Honor.**[105] So that this thing, who took such importance in the eyes of the person, is reduced to the nil (*fân*) and would not be associated to what we design as being *jamâl*.

What is *al-jamâl*?

This is the degree of the light which includes the apparent form and not the apparent form itself. Thus, there is not an only thing in the existence which does not have a

....

104 Surah at-Talaq, verse 3.
105 Surah ar-Rahman, verse 25.

specific luminous degree (*martabat nuraniya*), a luminous degree corresponding to a name between names of Allâh ﷻ.

The names of Allâh cannot be enumerated and are knew only by the Named ﷻ. It is Him who is the connoisseur of His essence, His attributes and His names. And can only really know this divine beauty people of the ultimate contemplation, those who recognize the forms no thanks to their appearances but the names whose they are the manifestations: people of the *dhikr*.

Some of them stuck to appearances and did not perceive the names whose they were the manifestations, and which animate their respective existences. It is in this that the knowledge of *al-qadar* is found.

As for those who, through *dhikr*, through the reality of the contemplative and the contemplated, grasped the *qadar* beyond the physical form of things, they knew its every move of these things. Their profound knowledge of the different apparent forms is based on their knowledge of the degrees of luminosity of these things and thus on the names that manifest themselves through them. The deeper meanings of these names are the truth of what appears of things.

Because, regarding what concerns Him (*huw*) or what concerns the reading of "*lahu*", it is about the absolute existence which could not be limited to a deeper meaning (*ma'na*) nor to a role (*cha'n*) nor to a status (*hukm*) nor to anything which can be expressed (*i'tibar*).

On the contrary, the whole of these degrees is in fact included and merged in His existence without distinction or prevalence of any of them over any other. His existence is an absolute and total existence. An exclusivity, without multiplicity, without duality. If we say that Allâh is unique (*wahid*), He is unique but in a dimension which, in fact, include the multiplicity, which include the second or the duality. In contrast, concerning al-Ahad (the Exclusive), it is a dimension that cannot tolerate any second.

These appearances – that means the whole of all these things—are established in the divine science without being considered as existing. Rather they are parts of nothingness, which the True ﷻ knows.

And if, in your pathway, you are from those who base their intellects, you imagine that you established a *'aqida* with your Lord, a *'aqida* based obviously on their belief in a divine transcendence (*tanzih*) pure and immaculate. The truth is that you swim in an ocean of analogy (*tachbîh*) and doubts (*tachkîk*). You are not in the state of nearness but rather in the state of lingering, because of your own existence, which you have not been able to deny and this in spite of the fact that the True ﷻ is such that, if you truly return to Him, you realize that He has erased you, even before you came into existence, and that it was through your extinction (fanâ') that He made you appear.

The appearances of the world are the vaults (*khazâ'in*) of the divine names and the divine names are the jewels they contain. Allâh ﷻ says: **And of everything, we hold the storehouses (*khazâ'in*).**[106] So the thing is by nature the deep meaning (*ma'nâ*) of a name from among the names of Allâh ﷻ. The completeness (*kamâl*) and the reservations (*khazâ'in*) of this name are the appearances through which it manifests itself to mankind and to all creatures. And had it not been for these *khazâ'in*, the names would never have

....

106 Surah al-Hijr, verse 21.

entered into appearance, while remaining in exclusive and absolute existence (*al-wujûd al-ahadiy*).

Allâh ❀ says: **And of everything, we hold the store-houses (*khazâ'in*), and We send it down only in a determined quantity (*qadar*).**[107]

The *qadar*, it is the apparent form of things. When you see a form—whatever the form—know that it is the *qadar* that permit you to see it. As for the spirits of these things or of these apparent forms, there are the divine names.

If for example, we talk about someone and that he is not present with us then it is like if his *qadar* was not present with us or to take another example, the case of the pregnant woman, we say that she carries a foetus in her belly. But in fact, Allâh knows better if the *qadar* of this new human being will come down and will take shape: **We send it down only in a determined quantity (*qadar*).** Understand that this baby to be born wear a name between names of Allâh ❀ as well as you and the whole of creation.

....
107 *Ibid.*

Ask yourself accounts...

And so, it is... even in the grave, he will come to you and when he presents himself to you, you will show *adab* regarding him. Do not imagine that the *hajir* who will come to you is someone that you do not know and that you will have to learn to know him once in the grave. No, the one who will come, it is necessarily someone you already know. When you take an exam, you will do it with the one with whom you learnt. If you had mathematics study, you would not see a philosophy's teacher to let you take the exam!

Scientists take their exams with scientists, and philosophers with philosophers. That's how it works. You, you study esoteric science (*al-'ilm al-laduni*). So, bring your science and let me take your exam! Or you hope someone will come to let you take the exam!? You do the *dhikr* waiting that at the end al-Khidr will come to take you the exam? No! Al-Khidr came to take the exam to *sayiduna* Musa (*'alayhi salâm*).

As for you, it is with your Shaykh that you are dealing with! So, this sanctified nature, if you did not understand it here, you will understand it on the day of the exam. If you do not understand the lesson in the classroom, you will understand it on the day of the test, *ya habibi*...

As mentioned it in the hadith: "*When the Lord will manifest Himself to people (worshippers) of fire by the fire*" that means that this fire that they adore, this fire which was their *hajir* in this world, it is him who will take them their exam in the Last Day.

And for people (worshippers) of 'Uzayr, He will manifest Himself as 'Uzayr. The one they loved besides Allâh, in him Allâh will manifest Himself to them and so on, until only the believers remain.

As for those who have worked on the *'aqidah* of *laysa kamithlihi chay*[108]: "He will manifest Himself to them, laughing (*wa huwa yadhak*)". Why will He laugh? Will there be a comedy show to laugh at!? No... of course not.

When you hear *wa huwa yadhak*, know that you will cry. Because the Lord assemble the opposite. It is Him who make cry and make laugh. Know that when he laughs, you will cry. Then He will talk to them and will tell them: "*What are you waiting?*" and they will answer: "*We are waiting our Lord!*" ... The Lord asks you what you are waiting for and you, you answer Him that you are waiting the Lord! And here is your *ma'rifa*... disappeared! As for Him, He will consider you according to the answer that you will give Him.

Be careful, what we are evoking here, it is in the *Sahih al-Bukhariy*... to know let you tell me that it is not authentical, not this or not that. *Sahih*... al-Bukhariy *radia Allâhu 'anhu*! And al-Bukhâriy refused to take a hadith from the one who made his horse believe that he had food so that it would come to him... so understand what it means *Sahih al-Bukhariy*.

"Do you have a sign with Him, which would allow you to recognize Him?" ... "Ah but these people told me... and

....

108 There is nothing like His example.

I read on book that..." No! Do you have, with you, something which is concrete!? Show us what you have! So, at this moment, what will you be able to show Him? Will you be able to take out your Islamic studies syllabus? Or open your schoolbag and take out the *Sahîh al-Bukhâriy* and *Muslim*? No! Open your heart and take out the book that is in it!

"Do you see a sign with Him?"... what will be your sign? It is the Light of Allâh! And then the Light of Allâh will manifest to every muslim. All muslims, without exception, who will be still there, waiting... they will see on this Day the Light of Allâh included the hypocrites!

Why even the hypocrites? Because they did not believe in it in this world. The Lord will let them see so that they believe in it. So, they will see it then Allâh will turn off their light and He will let it to muslims.

It is then that the Muslims will pass the *sirat*. The believers will be divided into two groups: the first to cross will be the group whose faces (*wujûh*)—and the face of the believer is his heart—will be like the moon when it is full. That is to say, those here who see the light of Allâh like a full moon are the people of the first group, those who will cross the *sirât* at the speed of lightning. Hell will say to them: "*O believer, cross quickly, because your light extinguishes my fire.*" Your light... not you! The hell does not fear you... you, you are nothing.

Then, the second group to cross are those who see a light similar to the brightest star in the sky. That means this star that you receive at the *bay'a*. So, on this Day... do not you realize that the Lord will give you the same *bay'a*? This same *bay'a* that you have taken here, the Lord will manifest Himself to you on the Last Day, laughing, and He will make you see the light. It means that Allâh will project His light into your heart, and some will then see it as the moon when it is full, while others will see it as the brightest star in the sky.

It is not exactly the same scenario that repeats itself!

People of the first group will cross "at lightning speed" that means that the space will fold up and you, here, do not you say that you too, are running at an extraordinary speed. You see worlds, you see galaxies... is not space folded up to you too!? You do not even consider darkness anymore, you flee in a tunnel, in a tube, in concentric waves of lights. You move away with an extraordinary speed... is not that so!?

Ask! Interrogate people to whom the Light of the Lord is manifesting! Those one, they will cross without any judgement! Why without any judgement?

Because in this world, they were among those who asked account to themselves. This world, they asked themselves accounts before they were asked. What they did here, it is over. We will not repeat the exercise to them in the hereafter. They already did it, so it is over for them, everything is ready.

As for the others, those who did not ask themselves for account in this world, they will have to do it hereafter. And how will they be held accountable? They will cross the *sirat* and when they will put the feet on it, Allâh will turn off their light because they did not rely on the light of the Lord! Rather, they rested on their own works, their memorization of the *Sahîh al-Bukhâriy* and *Muslim*... so-and-so had memorized the Qur'an, **like the donkey that carries leaves**[109]... he had even memorized its various readings, **and likewise,**

....
109 Surat al-Jumu'a, verse 5.

we install it in the hearts of criminals. It is then that the hooks will spring up, which will catch the feet of people.

What are these hooks?

These are all the multiplicities that you carry in consideration in yourself. You have them in your prayer, in your zakat, in your fasting. It is your ostentation, your vanity, your jealousy.

This person will pass and will be caught by all these hooks. We do not say that he will necessarily fall, nor that he will manage to cross. His fate is in the hands of Allâh. The fate of these Muslims is not clear. The only thing which is clear, it is the fate of the first and the second group who will cross that without rendering of accounts.

As for the others, if Allâh wants it, He saves them from the fire and if He wants it, He imposes them rendering of accounts on each of their work and then they fall into the fire.

Here is the meaning of "*He will manifest himself to them, laughing (wa huwa yadhak)*".

In this world, they made fun of Him... and in the Hereafter, He will make fun of them. In this world, they twisted the understandings of the Qur'an. They did not accept the rules as they are and, in the hereafter, the Lord will make them accountable.

Annihilate yourself in the Shaykh

Know, ô disciple, that the ultimate vision of the Prophet ﷺ consist by contemplating his luminous reality and not wanting to contemplate His corporal image like if you see your brother or your friend. This is a huge lack of convenience regarding the essence.

There are those among the people who relate the details of the vision of the Messenger of Allâh ﷺ by describing his features, his hair etc but this remains only imagination. The *tanazul* (descent) of the Prophet ﷺ into the *malakut* (spiritual world) remains light.

And when the Prophet ﷺ manifests himself to one of you, the certainty precedes his vision it means that the disciple will know beforehand that it is the Prophet ﷺ and not someone else because there is no being who can appear in his place.

As for the *awliyas* (saints), they appear as the shadow of the prophet because he is the true light. In this sense, he says ﷺ: "*I am leaving behind two things. You will never go astray as long as you hold fast onto them: the book of Allâh and the itraa of Ahlu Bayt (the family and the descendant of the Prophet).*"[110] This *itraa*, represented by children of the prophet linked to each other, enter through the *sanad* of the *silsila* (authentical chain).

....

110 *Sahih* Muslim.

Therefore, everything that the disciple acquires in terms of knowledge comes from his Shaykh, the Prophet ﷺ and Allâh. The disciple, therefore, will only contemplate the blessed face of the Prophet ﷺ through the vision of his Shaykh to the Prophet ﷺ because he is his companion at all times. Thus, the one who has loved the *waliy*, has certainly loved Allâh because we cannot reach the Divine presence without having passed through the *wasita*.

We have to notice that the love is the reason of the creation. He does not limit himself the love of the ego, the wife and the work.

Allâh said: "*The servant does not draw near to Me with anything more loved to Me than the religious duties I have obligated unto him. And My servant continues to draw near to me with nafil (supererogatory) deeds until I Love him. When I Love him, I am his hearing with which he hears, and his sight with which he sees, and his hand with which he strikes...*"[111].

If you reach at the point where your view become the view of the Shaykh, your hearing, your hand, your feet, you would then be the beloved of Allâh. And if you reach to forget yourself and annihilate yourself in the Shaykh so that you take him as imam during your prayers, to remove from your heart the existence of your being and feeling only his presence in your prayer, at this moment, you would be, certainly, a beloved of Allâh. However, if you pretended to be imam forgetting your Shaykh, you will be out of suitability without even realizing it.

....

111 Hadith *qudsi* related by al-Bukhari.

Consider the mirror of your Shaykh, beware of your mirror of Iblis

As for Iblis, he is the one who dress (*yalbis*) the righteousness (*istiqama*) by his opposite. But let consider him too and give him his part in the mirror. Since we talk about the Shaykh as a mirror, we can do it too with Iblis since it is always about the shadow. So, we can say about him that he is also your mirror.

Here is why the *ahl Allâh* and among them our Shaykh (*rahimahullâh*) always said that the Shaytân was like a cloth that we use to wipe things which are dirty in us. Thus, at each time you fall into one of your shortcomings, you say: "It is Iblis who did that..." No rather say: "I did that to myself". It is better. Do not need to bring Iblis and talk about him like that.

Now, if we take him as a mirror, if you attached yourself to him, to his tough, to his insufflations, take him and consider him as your mirror. Iblis is your mirror but not like the mirror of the Shaykh! The mirror of the Shaykh lets you see your inner self and the fruit of your vision of the Shaykh is that you reap the Light of the Lord ﷻ from it, you take the movements of the Star and the divine theophanies but what are you going to take on the mirror of Iblis?

Given that the work of Iblis consists by donning the things and give fake appearances. He will always let you perceive things to opposite of what they are really. And this state of righteousness when Iblis dress with it at his way, if you insist to observe him, you will see that things are inversed.

For example, when you are facing the mirror, observing yourself, these eyes you see disposed like they are, if you look carefully, you will realize that they are inversed. As for the mirror of the Shaykh, he does not return you your own image. Rather, he is returning the image of you who travel through the *qibla* of *sayiduna* al-Mustafa ﷺ.

So, if you look in the mirror of the Shaykh, you will see your neck. And if you look in the mirror of the Shaytân, you will see as in the mirror of your bathroom. That means that you will see that everything is inversed but not inversed in the sense where your head is down and your feet are up, rather that all things which are in the right appear in the left and all things which are in the left appear in the right. As well as this mirror has the faculty to inverse the apparent forms, he inverses the thoughts, the intentions, the knowledge and the way to consider these revealed Sciences. These theophanies are obviously pure free of any falsification except if you dress yourself these realities with false appearances!

How can it be possible? With your bad thoughts. And where do they come from these bad thoughts? On your inner self, because the *qarin* circulates in the veins of each person. From there, you will begin to do unfounded interpretations, stupid, based on wrong appearances like if you were bewitched. This is the expertise of Iblis. If you want to know Iblis and you need obligatory this knowledge here, if you want to be able to clean and purify your *moustaqarr*.

If you do not know your enemy's weapons and methods of action, he will eventually defeat and subdue you.

Only here, we barely mention the name of Iblis, people are scared and step back. But no! You have to learn to know who is Iblis in order is to be able to defeat him, with the strength of the luminous Faith. If you just settle for fleeing as soon as you hear the name of Iblis, the least little torment will cause you a great harm.

All the expertise of Iblis consists of making the false true and the true false. He ended up to the point where the witchcraft is considered as the religion and the religion as the witchcraft. Here is Iblis.

We are at the point where, at the end of the times, when you say **Allâh is the Light of the heavens and the earth**[112], we come to tell you "No, this light, it is a manifestation of Iblis". Why? Because they inversed all the comprehensions. He makes you see the religion in the appearance of the witchcraft and the witchcraft – meaning the darkness – he makes you see them in the appearance of the Light. It is this way Iblis acts with you. And you came to the point to love the darkness instead of the Light. Instead of running away and go to flee in the Light, you run away the Light to flee in the darkness...

....

112 Surah an-Nur, verse 35.

Erase yourself without
the slightest hint of existence

The one who ware (*al-saqiy*) is anyone else except the one who drink (*al-charib*) himself. The wine come up in you, through you and it get drunk in you by yourself. Then do not remain about him except the name while you, you are his deep and pre-eternal sense.

But how would you be, you, the deep sense of the name?

If you consider the name in his written form (*mastur*), you have to taste the reality of the lecture of the *hâ* by his ten degrees. Then, you will get striped by your own body, your attributes, your apparent form, your name and finally your spirit could be seized (*qabd*) absolutely and definitively so that it does not remain anything else except the footstep of yourself.

However, if it remains any footstep of yourself, your movements become at this moment absolute movements (*itlaq*) and your characteristics become highly celestial characteristics.

Thus, you will become "*ama*" and from this "*ama*" will appear the absolute nature of the name Allâh. This is because your only goal was to return to the reality of the Divine Order (*al-haqîqa al-amriya*), and thus to the knowledge of the Lord (*ma'rifat al-rubûbiya*) and when this name is split (*inshaqqa*)... where will you be? You will be in the *fasl* who is the absolute *"ama"* then it will be like if you were in the *barzakh* of this *lâm al-qabd*.

Since this spiritual station, *sayiduna* Sulayman (*ʿalayhi salam*) says: **Grant me a kingdom such as will not belong to anyone after me.**[113] That means that he asked for the *mulk* of the ultimate essence (*al-dhât al-ʾaliya*) and did not simply stick to the multiple names and attributes. So that everything ended up turning and referring to him and he saw absolutely nothing, neither before him nor after him.

That means that when the person accesses to this spiritual sanctified dimension (*hadra aqdasiya*), he does not see nor consider anymore any forms of others. There is only an erasure complete and definitive in the presence of the True. There is no more before, nor after, because the individual then lost time, his being and all that could be able to reveal him a pronoun whatever it is. There is no more for him neither pronoun, nor appearance. Rather, he has only *huwa*, such as **nothing is like His example** the Unique, Exclusive, Singular, the Only One to be considered.

The holder if this contemplative state does not see any more anyone else accept himself as well as before than after him. Rather, he is the existence past and future. To his eyes, the pre-eternity and the eternity do not distinguish between them, it is the total liberty: **This is Our gift, so grant or withhold without account.**[114] Among the things that are part of his *mulk*, the capacity to order the wind. Because as soon as he realized his extinction (*fana'*) without coming back, he became as the water which goes in everything even

....

113 Surah Sad, verse 35.
114 Surah Sad verse 39.

to the point to circulate in the air, in the objects. It had not colour nor form. Among the characteristics of his *mulk* also, the fact to visit one hundred wives in the same night, what is humanly impossible.

According to Abu Hureira: "*Sulaymân son of Dâwûd ('alayhi salâm) says: "I will visit this night one hundred women, each of them will put in the world a boy who will fight in the path of Allâh. The angel tells him: "Say insha Allâh!" but he did not say it. Indeed, he visited these wives but only one of them gave birth and then to a half-man.*"

This hadith is authentic, reported by al-Bukhâriy in his *Sahih*. No default can be found to this story, it is unquestionable.

So, we have a man, a human being, who visits one hundred women in one night. Even if... even if you will imagine that the Lord would not give him the physical strength of a such thing... how to do this within the time limit of a single day? Twelve hours would not be enough, not even twenty-four. For that, you need longer hours than the known ones.

So here, you taste to the speed of the folding (*al-tayy*) of the time and the space. This capacity (*qudra*) appears to you like coming from the Truth ﷻ by manifesting himself to one of His creatures that He prepared and shaped to accomplish that.

Because as soon as the individual became entirely erased without the slightest hint of existence. He can, effectively, cross the time and the space and so to accomplish the things that cannot accomplish the one who remain linked to the chains of spatial directions, to the chains of the place where he is captive, to the chains of the nil!

Conclusion

We hope that we succeeded to share with you as much as possible the sense of our Shaykh's words, that you tasted the flavour of his wisdoms and that you felt the perfume of the presence like we felt it during all the reminders of our Shaykh Sidi Mohamed Faouzi al-Karkari, may Allâh sanctify his secret.

We would like to thank each person who participated in any way in the development of this publication.

We ask Allâh to forgive us our failure regarding Him and His creatures. May Allâh illuminate our heart and our mind by the company of the knower of Allâh, sidi Mohamed Faouzi al-Karkari, may Allâh sanctify his secret, until we reach our form in His form, our names in His name, our essence in His essence.

Ô Allâh, count us among people of your presence, among those that You certified and loved. Count us among the worshipper of your commitment and permit to our heart to receive the rain of your blessings.

Ô Allâh, perfect our behaviour, our education and our conveniences until we become the shadow of the Beloved, *sayiduna* al-Mustafa ﷺ.

Ô Allâh, we ask you to make this publication an act who's only motivation would be Your face and if our intention is corrupted, we invoke you to accept this correction.

Ô Allâh, give us the strength to serve You without any request from us, to love You without looking for Your love, to adore You without fear of Your hell or desire of Your paradise.

You know how much we sinned and how much we disobey to Your Order, cover us with the veil of the merciful and gather us under the shadow of Your throne on the day when there will be no shadow. We implore Your nearness by the blessed Names of the tree and count us, Ô Lord, among Your near ones.

Glossary

Adab	The rules of propriety. It refers to prescribed Islamic etiquette: good manners, morals, decorum, decency, humaneness
Adhan	Islamic call to prayer
'Arif	The real knower
Asma' al-husna	Names of Allâh
'Asr	Islamic prayer
Athar of the risala	Means vestige of the message
Award	Plurial of *wird*, it is a regular litany and a mystical invocation practiced by *murids* in islamic sufism
Baraka	Blessing
Barzakh	in the meaning of isthmus
Basira	Heart's vision
Caïn	Name of the son of the prophet Adam (*'alayhi salam*)
Da'wa	It is the act of inviting or calling people to embrace Islam
Dhawq	The flavour

Dhikr	It means literally "reminder" or "mention". It is a form of Islamic meditation in which phrases or prayers are repeatedly chanted in order to remember God. The content of the prayers includes the names of God or a *dua* (prayer of supplication) taken from the hadiths or the Quran.
Dhohr	Islamic prayer
Du'a	Invocation, supplication or request asking help or assistance from God
Dunia	The lowest world
Fana	Evanescence, ceasing to exist, annihilation, complete denial of self and the realization of God that is one of the steps taken by the Muslim Sufi (mystic) toward the achievement of union with God.
Faqih	Disciple
Fasiq	The pervert
Fiqh	It is Muslim jurisprudence
Fu'âd	Depth of the heart
Ghafil	Reckless
Ghafla	Carelessness
Ghayb	The domain of unknown, the unsee. It refers to that which is absent, hidden, concealed
Ghusl	The "major ablution" that entails washing the entire body in ritually pure water
Hadra	It means presence but it is also collective supererogatory ritual performed by Sufi orders

Haqiqa	The truth
Haqq	The Truth
Hasana	The good deeds
Hâtif	The divine inspiration
Ichara	Sign
Idhn	The authorization
Ihsân	The perfection
Ijtihad	It is an Islamic legal term referring to independent reasoning or the thorough exertion of a jurist's mental faculty in finding a solution to a legal question
Imân	The faith
'Isha	Islamic prayer
Jalâl	Divine majesty
Jamal	Divine beauty
Janâba	Impure state
Kachf	Unveiling
Khalwa	Spiritual retirement
Khidma	The work
Khushû'	The fear
Kufr	The miscreant
Maqam	Spiritual station
Ma'rifa	Divine knowledge, esoteric knowledge
Markaz	Center
Michkat	The recess

Mi'raj	Nightly ascent
Mulk	The sensorial world perceptible by the five senses
Muraqa'a	Multicolor *djelabah* used by Karkary's disples
Murid	The disciple
Mushahada	The state of wakefulness
Mustaqarr	Receptacle
Naba'	Great news
Nafs	It can be translated by "ego"
Nawâfil	It is a type of optional Muslim *salah* (formal worship). As with sunna prayer, they are not considered obligatory but are thought to confer extra benefit on the person performing them
Noubouwa	The prophecy
Qabd	The state of oppression
Qabda	The handful
Qadar	It s the concept of divine destiny in Islam
Qârin	It is the Shaytân associated to each human being
Qotb	The pole
Rahman	The Merciful
Rak'at	It is a single iteration of prescribed movements and supplications performed by Muslims as part of the prayer known as *salah*
Rassul	The prophet

Risala	Message
Risala	The message
Saqar	The fourth degree of the Hell
Shahada	The testimony and it refers to te Muslim pro-fession of faith: "There is no god but God; Muhammad is the Prophet of God."
Shari'a	The Islamic laws
Silsila	It means the authentical chain. It may be translated as "spiritual genealogy" where one Sufi Master transfers his *khilfat* to his spiri-tual descendant
Sirr	The secret
Sobh	The Islamic prayer of the sunrise
Sufli	Concerning what is low
Taghut	The Arabic *taghut* is variously interpreted to refer to idols, a specific tyrant, an oracle or an opponent of the Prophet. "The believers fight for God's cause, while those who reject faith fight for an unjust cause (*taghut*)
Tajrid	It is the fact to live and stay with the company of the Shaykh
Tariqa	The Muslim spiritual path toward direct knowledge (*ma'rifah*) of God or Reality (*Haqq*). *Tariqa* came to mean the order itself
Tawba	The repentance
Tawhid	The Unicity, the oneness of God, in the sense that He is one and there is no god but He

Tawwakul	Islamic concept of the reliance on God or "trusting in God's plan". It is seen as "perfect trust in God and reliance on Him alone."
Tayammum	It is the Islamic act of dry ablution using sand or dust, which may be performed in place of ritual washing if no clean water is readily available or if one is suffering from moisture-induced skin inflammation or scaling
Wasita	Intermediary
Waswas	In Islam, it refers to whispers from Shaytân
Zawiya	The Shaykh's home

At the Service of Destiny

*A Biography of the Living Moroccan Sufi Master
Shaykh Mohamed Faouzi al-Karkari*

....

In the Footsteps of Moses

*A Contemporary Sufi Commentary on the Story of
God's Confidant (kalīm Allāh) in the Qur'ān*

....

Sufism Revived

*A Contemporary Treatise on Divine Light,
Prophecy and Sainthood*

....

The Foundations
of the Karkariya Order

....

Introduction
to Islamic Metaphysics

*A Contemporary Sufi Treatise on the Secrets
of the Divine Name*

Printed and bound
in the United States of America

www.ingramcontent.com/pod-product-compliance
Lightning Source LLC
LaVergne TN
LVHW091704190726
843493LV00001B/144